WORD
·PLAY·

WORD
PLAY

Brian Bamber & Roger Bowers

WORD ·PLAY·

Longman

Longman Group UK Limited
Harlow and London
Associated companies, branches,
and representatives throughout the world

© Longman Group Limited 1990

First published by Longman Group Limited 1990
Second impression 1991

ISBN 0 582 00535 3

Produced by Longman Group (FE) Ltd
Printed in Hong Kong

INTRODUCTION

Word Play is a source book for intermediate and advanced students of English and their teachers. It can be used in a classroom setting or for private study. The book has no explicit syllabus, functional or formal, but aims through the stimulation of language use to develop the **lexical command** and the **sociocultural awareness** of the learner.

Word Play is a collection of 350 activity questions. Each question provides the starting point for an investigation into English vocabulary. In a classroom situation, the questions can also be a stimulus to group activity and discussion, followed by teacher consolidation if desired. A full key is provided which offers background information to the teacher or alternatively serves as a reference source for students. The questions range from the brief to the very brief. Many contain elements of humour, curiosity or play upon words. They focus upon features unlikely to be covered by normal course texts – homophones and homonyms, lexical sets, collocations, idiomatic usage and stylistic variation, sociocultural contexts beyond the 'core' situations of family, education, work, pastimes, etc.

The book also provides opportunities for learners, working on their own or in class, to make full use of their dictionaries in seeking solutions to the puzzles which are set. The **key** incorporates definitions, characterizations and inventories of acceptable items based on the *Longman Dictionary of Contemporary English* (LDOCE) and the *Longman Lexicon of Contemporary English* (LLOCE).

Word Play is not directed towards learners from any specific linguistic or cultural background. It may even be used with enjoyment by interested native speakers of English.

The question types include:

A PARTS OF WORDS
in which affixes are provided with cues for their inclusion in a range of words: e.g. *Think of as many words as you can which end in – ship but have nothing to do with water.*

B SETS OF WORDS
in which distinctions must be made between words within
a given lexical set: e.g. *Explain the differences between
the words below: notice, glimpse, view, stare at, glare at,
catch sight of*

C WORDS INTO PHRASES
in which a single lexical item must be used within a
selection of phrases, often with a wide variety of
meanings: e.g. *What colour can you add to the words
below to make new ones?: belt, fingers, horn, house, light,
room*

D PLAYING WITH WORDS
comprising a range of word games, including word
squares, word chains, word links, hidden words, odd
man out, etc: e.g. *Think of a word meaning rubbish which
sounds like one referring to part of the human body.*

E IDIOM AND IMAGERY
in which expressions employing idiomatic imagery are
presented for interpretation: e.g. *What happened to Fred
when he kicked the bucket?*

F COLLOCATIONS
Groupings of words which, through common usage,
naturally go together, and where substitution of individual
words is not normally acceptable: e.g. *Which preposition
can you use with marry in this sentence? "Humphrey is
married to/with/by my sister Julie."*

G CULTURAL CUES
Items specific to the culture underlying British English, for
interpretation and possible comparison with usage in
other cultures: e.g. *How might you address the following
people or groups in a formal situation?: the audience, an
ambassador, a prince or princess, a president, a prime
minister?*

A Think of as many words as you can which end in **-ship** but have nothing to do with water, and then write sentences showing how each word is used. If you are working in a group, score one point for each word none of the other groups thought of, plus one more point for each word you have used correctly in a sentence.

B Match the names of these tools to their pictures on the right.

chisel
screwdriver
mallet
plane
pliers

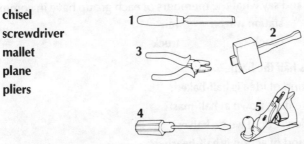

C Suggest situations, giving examples, of ways in which these phrases might be used.

pull a fast one   **pull a face**
pull rank   **pull someone/something to pieces**
pull your weight   **pull someone's leg**

D How can you get from **sick** to **well** by changing one letter at a time? (Each move must produce an English word, of course!)

Answer: sick   silk   sill   will   well

Now try getting from **cold** to **warm** in the same way.

E What kind of person would you call **butterfingers**?

F Which preposition can you use with **marry** in this sentence?

                           to
Humphrey is **married   with** my sister Julie.
                           by

G **Time, gentlemen, please!** What time?

A Think of as many words as you can which begin with **inter-**, and then write sentences showing how each word is used. If you are working in a group, score one point for each word none of the other groups thought of, plus one more point for each word you have used correctly in a sentence.

B Which of the following go together? Make two or three groups of words and say what the members of each group have in common.

car   station wagon   van
lorry   coach   truck

C What is **half the battle**?

What kind of idea is **half-baked**?

Why are flags flown at **half-mast**?

What do we do if we go **halves**?

What kind of action is **half-hearted**?

D Use the letters given below to complete this crossword by making three words across from left to right and three more words down from top to bottom.

A   B   C   D   D   E   O   O

	N	

E What happened to Fred when he **kicked the bucket**?

F When something goes wrong with a machine and it stops working, is it **out of order**, **out of work**, or **out of the question**?

G When would you be most likely to hear this phrase used?

... in sickness or in health ...

A   How many of the verbs below make a new word if you add the
ending -ment?

arrange	remove	repeat
attach	entertain	judge
destroy	bewilder	amuse
collect	astonish	replace
excite	decide	wonder

B   In Britain you can eat and drink in a **cafe**, a **restaurant**, and
sometimes in a **pub**. Do you know what the difference is?

C   What is a **hard-and-fast** rule?
How do you cook a **hard-boiled** egg?
What do we mean when we say that someone is **hard-boiled**?
Where would you find the **hard shoulder**?
What is a **hardback**?
Are you **hard of hearing**?

D   Some word endings (suffixes) can also be used at the beginnings
of words (prefixes). For example, **nail** may be added to the end of
the word **finger** or to the beginning of the word **brush**, to make the
new words **fingernail** and **nailbrush**.
Can you find one word which can connect **writing** and **knife** in the
same way?

E   Have you ever **carried something too far**? What does this expression
mean?

F   Choose **make** or **do** in each of the following sentences:
I can't come just yet. I have to **make/do** the washing up.
The children were **making/doing** faces at the other car drivers.
I didn't have time to **make/do** the bed before I went to work.
Jessica decided to have nothing more to **make/do** with George.
We're staying late at the office to **make/do** the accounts.

4

A Think of one prefix which can be used to make new words out of the words below, and then write as many sentences as you can using at least three of the words.

break	rage	burst	rank	wards
class	set	dated	side	post
door	law	going	standing	right
lay	spoken	point	cast	skirts

B How might you **catch: your breath, your death, it**, and **someone out**?

C What colour can you add to the words below to make new ones?

belt   **fingers**   **horn**   **house**   **light**

What do the new words mean?

D Can you think of a word meaning 'rubbish' which sounds the same as a word referring to 'part of the human body'?

E Where in a house might you find a **head** and a **foot**? Where else?

F Which of the following expressions is incorrect, and what should it be?

She goes to work
- by bus
- by train
- by taxi
- by foot
- by car

G What have these places in common?

hostel   **hall of residence**   **bed-sitter**   **home**

A   Think of as many words as you can beginning with **self-**, and then write sentences showing how each word is used. If you are working in a group, score one point for each word none of the other groups thought of, plus one more for each word you have used correctly in a sentence.

B   What have these in common?
    club   **diamond**   **heart**   **spade**

C   Think of four sentences using the word **ground** in different senses.

D   Think of a word meaning 'heaviness' which sounds the same as one meaning 'don't go away'.

E   When might you be asked to **hold your tongue**?

F   Which preposition can you use with **reason** in this sentence?

                    to
    What is the reason **of**   his disgrace?
                    for

G   **8 ... 9 ... 10 ... out!**
    If someone is saying this to you, you probably don't feel very well. Why?

6

A   Think of as many words as you can which begin with **sub-**, and then write sentences showing how each word is used. If you are working in a group, score one point for each word none of the other groups thought of, plus one more point for each word you have used correctly in a sentence.

B   Who sits on the **front bench**?

Who is in the **front line**?

Why might you **hold the front page**?

Who is the **front-runner**?

C   Make sense of the following rhyme by adding appropriate punctuation.

I saw a man jump over a house
I saw the moon beneath the sea
I saw a fish driving a car
I saw the Queen upon a bike
I saw a girl within a glass
I saw the one who saw all this.

D   What would you be doing if you were **flogging a dead horse**?

E   How many combinations of these words could be used to fill the blanks in the sentence below?

call   put   end   stop   halt

I'm determined to . . . a(n) . . . to this silliness.

F   Find the missing words:

ready, steady, ...

red, amber, ...

Tom, Dick and ....

lock, stock and ....

Suggest situations in which these phrases might be used.

G   Who is the **best man** at a wedding? What is his task?

A What do the following words mean?

short circuit **shortfall** **shortbread**
shortcoming **short list** **shorthand**

B How many different kinds of literary writing, such as a **novel** or **poem**, can you think of?

C How would you use the following expressions?

like a fish out of water
have other fish to fry
fishing for compliments
to sound or smell fishy

D John **married** Peter and his sister.

If no laws were broken, what can you say about John?

E If I'm making a great effort to do something, what part of my body do I **put into** it?

F Which preposition can you use with **congratulations** in this sentence?

> **at**
> Congratulations **for** winning the scholarship.
> **on**

G What would happen if you pulled the **communication cord** in a British train, and when might you do so?

8

A What do the following words mean?

double bass   **double bed**   **double-decker**
doubles   **double-edged**   **double-glazing**

B Find as many words as you can which mean the opposite of **new**, **young** and **modern**. Provide sentences giving contexts. Look for special meanings. For example, when may **full** be the opposite of **new**? What are the restrictions on **ancient**?

C Which word would complete all of these sentences?

John was **on top of the** ....
Mary **thinks the** .... **of** Stephen.
I thought the film was **out of this** ....
What in the .... is the answer?

D Get from **fish** to **meat** by changing one letter at a time.

E What are **crocodile tears**?

F Which of these sentences is incorrect and why?

We had a discussion about students' grants.
We discussed about students' grants.

G What letters are used to represent musical notes?

A Explain these terms.

cold-blooded   **cold-hearted**   **cold feet**   **cold shoulder**

B Name as many colours as you can.

C Which word would complete all of these sentences?

Think .... **of it.**

It cost **next to** ....

There's .... **for it** now.

I'll **do** .... **of the kind.**

That's .... **to do with** me.

You ain't .... **but a hound dog.**

D Get from **gold** to **bell** one letter at a time.

E According to the proverb, what kind of **horse** should you not **look in the mouth** of?

F Write sentences to show the differences in meaning between the following verbs.

dress   **dress in**   **dress up**

G Why be careful on April 1st?

10

A How many words can you add to **high-** to give special meanings?

B What do these crimes involve?
  arson   theft   burglary
  fraud   embezzlement   treason

C What can you **keep, break, eat, be taken at** and **be as good as**?

D What is the longest word in the English language? (Hint: Don't go metric!)

E If my mind turns to **another kettle of fish**, is it because I'm hungry?

F How are the following verbs used in the sentences below?
  pay for   pay off   pay up   pay into

  When she realized she had to return the money she decided to .... at once.

  If you wish, we can .... the money straight .... your account.

  If you supply the food, I'll .... the drinks.

  His work was terrible, so after a week we decided to .... him ....

G Where would you live if you were of **no fixed abode**?

A   Which word would complete all these sentences?

If you misbehave I'll **give** you **what** ....

You'll **be** .... **it**.

There's gratitude .... **you**.

If it weren't .... **you**, we wouldn't be in this mess!

B   Name some other areas of water of these kinds.

pond   stream

C   What can you **kill, pass, do** (we hope you won't), **spend**, and **waste**?

D   What is an **IOU**?

E   Am I uncomfortable if I'm **full of beans**?

F   Which of these sentences are acceptable and which are not?

I tried to explain the meaning of the phrase to them.

I tried to explain them the meaning of the phrase.

What explanation on this can you offer?

What explanation of this can you offer?

G   **Great Britain** and the **United Kingdom**: what's the difference?

A   List as many words as you can ending in **-ology**. Then you will have your personal **-ology** anthology!

B   Say what you know about these creatures.

    fairy   witch   wizard   gnome   dwarf   goblin

C   You **make me** ....

    I'm .... **and tired of** your nonsense.

    I'm **worried** .... about you.

    Well, what's the word?

D   Which words connect the following?

    a **typewriter** and a **prison**

    a **tree** and an **elephant**

    a **book** and a **knight**

    a **bicycle** and an **organ**

E   Why would you probably not be grateful if I gave you **a piece of my mind**?

F   Select the right word.

                    with

    She's very good **in**   tennis.

                    at

G   List what you would find on a university campus (apart from enlightenment).

A   Think of as many words as you can which begin with **mis-**, and then write sentences showing how each word is used. If you are working in a group, score one point for each word none of the other groups thought of, plus one more point for each word you have used correctly in a sentence.

B   Think of sentences to show how these words are used.

say   speak   tell

C   What substance will give you the answers to the following questions?

What sort of **fist** might you have **in a velvet glove**?

What would you do while this was **hot**?

Why might you **rule with a rod of** this?

Could you have a **curtain** made of this?

D   Many words have more than one meaning. For example, **well** may mean 'a hole in the ground' or 'not ill'. Can you think of one word which means both 'of high quality' and 'money paid as a punishment'?

E   Why shouldn't you want to **get into hot water**?

F   Choose the correct preposition.

        with
She spoke to the crowd **in**   a loud voice.
        on

G   When would you, and when would you not, say **bye-bye**?

14

A   Think of as many words as you can ending in **-ation**, and then write sentences showing how each word is used. If you are working in a group, score one point for each word none of the other groups thought of, plus one more point for each word you have used correctly in a sentence.

B   Think of sentences to show how these words are used.
   see   watch   look at

C   **Look** these terms **up**!
   What's he **up to**?
   Are you feeling **up to it**?
   What's **up**?

D   Say why, in your view, **knowledge** is like the following.
   a **candle**   a **road**   a **loaf of bread**   a **knife**

E   If I'm **boiling**, am I ready for a cup of tea?

F   How many combinations of the words given may fill the blanks in this sentence?
   close   **shut**   **end**   **window**
   meeting   **conversation**   **relationship**
   Ms Brown .... the .... at four o'clock.

G   Does a **bylaw** have anything to do with farewells?

A   List as many words as you can which can end in **-ism**, and write sentences showing how the words are used. If you are working in a group, score one point for each word no other group has thought of, plus one more point for each correct sentence.

B   What can you **turn on** and **off**?
What can you **switch on** and **off**?
What can you **open** and **close**?

C   What are the following?

open-and-shut case   **open season**   **open house**
open air   **open secret**   **open question**

D   Can you think of a word for 'physical' which can also refer to 'an army rank'?

E   Is it only the greengrocer who **knows** his **onions**?

F   Choose the appropriate prepositions:
Adrian may not be in love .... Julie, but he's certainly very fond .... her.

G   Where would you choose to sit in a theatre: **stalls, circle, gallery** or **box**? Why?

A List as many words as you can beginning with **in-**, and write sentences showing how the words are used. If you are working in a group, score one point for each word no other group has thought of, plus one more point for each correct sentence.

B Explain the differences between the words below.

notice	glimpse	view
stare at	glare at	catch sight of

C **Keep** your ....s **crossed**.

She has a .... **in every pie**.

I've been **working** my ....s to the bone.

Don't you dare **lay a** .... **on** him.

Mind you don't **burn** your ....s.

He can **twist** them **round** his **little** ....

It helps to have **the facts at** your ....**tips**.

I'm all ....s **and thumbs**.

D If we look carefully at certain sentences we can find hidden words. For example, **America** is hidden in: 'Where's the **jam?' Eric a**sked.

Now work in pairs to find three islands in the following sentences.

The first keeps its secret ever so well.

In the second you'll find an animal tamed.

You needn't feel badly about the third.

E What **keeps the doctor away**?

F Choose the correct preposition.

His loss was so great that even his enemies took pity

with
on him.
to

G What kinds of things could you buy at a **sweetshop** or **confectioner's**?

A Think of as many words as you can beginning with **re-**, and then write sentences showing how each word is used. If you are working in a group, score one point for each word none of the other groups thought of, plus one more point for each word you have used correctly in a sentence.

B Think up sentences to show how the words below are used.

thin   slim   slender   fine   narrow

C What word is missing from the following text?

There was no .... of a fuss when John, at a loose .... one week .... , jumped in at the deep .... 'This is the .... ,' said his mother. His uncle, getting the wrong .... of the stick, told him how brave he'd been.

D Find the three hidden animals.

The first would seem to be a Russian one.

I came late to find the second.

With the third we must stop, I gather.

E Is it a formal occasion if I **get all shirty**?

F Show how **moist, damp** and **humid** are used by fitting them into the appropriate sentences below:

If you wear those socks you'll catch a cold; they're ....

Kate took a bite of the rich, ... Christmas cake.

At this time of year the jungle is particularly hot and ....

G What sport, other than football, do these terms come from?

offside   foul   goal   half-time   penalty

18

A   Think of as many words as you can beginning with **pre-**, and then write sentences showing how each word is used. If you are working in a group, score one point for each word none of the other groups thought of, plus one more point for each word you have used correctly in a sentence.

B   Explain the differences between the words below.

job   **work**   **employment**   **profession**
vocation   **post**   **appointment**

C   Which word can go before the following to make new words?

speech   **hand**   **range**   **will**   **for-all**

D   Sarah and Sue had a walking match. They agreed to do six miles each along the road from London to Brighton. Sarah did the first stretch from the twelfth milestone to the sixth while Sue walked from the sixth milestone to the first. Sue won easily, even though her stretch of the road was more hilly. Was it a fair contest?

E   Apart from little boys, what else can **come in short pants**?

F   Which word fits the phrase?

It was late when their parents got back and the children were already **quick/fast** asleep.

G   What sounds can a car engine make?

A   How many of the following words can take the prefix **counter-**? Score one point for each correct word and minus one for each incorrect word.

point	**foil**	**claim**	**join**	**pour**
measure	**drink**	**know**	**blast**	
sign	**sing**	**tenor**	**soprano**	

B   What word is missing from the following text and what does it all mean?

He's so stubborn, he won't **budge an** .... But I can't give in to him, because if you **give** him **an** .... , he**'ll take a mile**.

C   How many words can you find which combine the word **black** with another word to give another meaning?

D   Can you find one word which links **rain** and **out** to make two new words in the same way as **nail** connects **finger** and **brush** to make **fingernail** and **nailbrush**?

E   Think of one word which can mean both 'to send a strong current of air' and also 'a hard stroke with the hand or a weapon'.

F   Which word fits the phrase?

I've been working since five o'clock this morning and I'm

tired
    out
    up .
    off

G   How many of the eight public holidays in England and Wales can you name? Do these include the **busman's holiday**?

A   Think of as many words as you can which begin with **dead**, and then write sentences showing how each word is used. If you are working in a group, score one point for each word none of the other groups thought of, plus one more point for each word you have used correctly in a sentence.

B   Express admiration in as many ways as you can.
e.g. 'How was the play?' '**Marvellous!**'

C   What word gives the answer to the following questions?

What does the dreamer have **in the clouds**?

If you're good in a crisis, what do you **keep**?

If a problem is finally unavoidable what has it **come to**?

Where must success not **go**?

D   'In my desk in the teachers' room,' said Mr Torquelott, 'I have some felt-tip pens – six yellow ones, eight red ones and twelve black ones. Go and get me three all of the same colour. Any colour will do.'

But when Polly got to the teachers' room there was a power cut and she couldn't see the colours. How many pens did she take back?

E   'He's **let himself go**' has a negative sense. 'Come on, **let yourself go**' has a positive one. Can you explain?

F   Choose the correct word.

The rainstorm caught us unawares and we were soaked to
the
    skin
    bone.
    hair

G   Which groups of people do the following words refer to?
delegation   **congregation**   **jury**
supporters   **audience**

A What do the words below have in common, and what do they mean?

hereafter   **hereby**   **herein**
heretofore   **hereupon**   **herewith**

B Explain the meanings of the words below. Can you **add** any more?

addition   **adjacent**   **adverse**
address   **advocate**   **adhere**

C Who **carries the can**?
Who **carries weight**?
Who **carries things too far**?

D Can you find one word which links **under** and **port** to make two new words in the same way as **nail** connects **finger** and **brush** to make **fingernail** and **nailbrush**?

E You may be able to **lead a horse to water** but what can't you make it do?

F Choose the correct word.

We've done everything we can. Now all we can do is hope for the best and keep our   **fingers**
  thumbs crossed.
  arms

G What does **C** mean when we are talking about temperature? What about **F**?

A Think of as many words as you can which begin with **head**, and then write sentences showing how each word is used. If you are working in a group, score one point for each word none of the other groups thought of, plus one more point for each word you have used correctly in a sentence.

B Label these parts of the car on the picture below.

bonnet	**windscreen**	**boot**	**hubcap**
bumper	**tyre**	**wing**	

C What word is missing from the following sentences?

It's enough to make your .... **stand on end**.

Come on, **let your** .... **down**.

She didn't **turn a** ....

Don't **split** ....s.

D Can you find one word which links **whole** and **thing** to make two new words in the same way as **nail** connects **finger** and **brush** to make **fingernail** and **nailbrush**?

E Think of one word which may mean 'a group of words' and 'a punishment'.

F Choose the appropriate phrase.

Grace appreciates most kinds of music, but jazz isn't really her **mug of coffee**   **glass of beer**   **cup of tea**.

G How are the words below used?

Oxbridge   **Oxon**   **Cantab**

A   Think of as many words as you can which begin with **hard**, and then write sentences showing how each word is used. If you are working in a group, score one point for each word none of the other groups thought of, plus one more point for each word you have used correctly in a sentence.

B   How and why would you make these noises?

a **hiccup**	a **sniffle**	a **sneeze**
a **cough**	**hm, hm**	**tut tut**

C   If you **fall foul of** someone, what do they think of you?

Have you ever told a joke which **fell flat**?

Is there something you'd **fall over backwards** to do?

D   Can you find one word which links **pass** and **play** to make two new words in the same way as **nail** connects **finger** and **brush** to make **fingernail** and **nailbrush**?

E   Where might **cats and dogs** come from if the sun wasn't shining?

F   In what contexts can each of the words below be the opposite of **sweet**?

sour   **savoury**   **bitter**   **dry**

G   What did **Peter Piper pick a peck of**?

A   Match the endings **-hood, -dom** and **-ness** to the beginnings below:
    official   like   likeli-   child   martyr   mean

B   In how many ways could you walk down a street? For example,
    you could **march**.

C   How many words can you think of which combine the word **blood**
    with another word to give new meanings?

D   Can you find one word which links **man** and **less** to make two new
    words in the same way as **nail** links **finger** and **brush** to make
    fingernail and **nailbrush**?

E   What, apart from food, might we wish to **take with a pinch of salt**?

F   Show how the words below may be used with 'torch', 'tea', 'ruler'
    and 'wrestler'. For example, tea can be **strong** but not **brawny**.
    strong   mighty   powerful   brawny

G   What are some of the things you would see at a **circus**?

A What do the words below mean? Can you think of at least five more words beginning with **down-**?

downstream   **downcast**   **downwind**
down-at-heel   **downfall**

B You open a cookery book and look at the recipes. How many different ways of cooking might it suggest?

C How many words can you think of which combine the word **first** with another word to give new meanings?

D Use the letters given below to create words down and across but not diagonally.

A   B   B   D   E   E   I   R

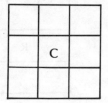

E What wouldn't you do to someone **as far as you could throw them**?

F Which number fits this particular phrase?

The sight was so astonishing that people came from the
three
four   corners of the earth to see it.
five

G How might you amuse yourself at a **funfair**?

A   Do you know what these are?

    grandfather clock   **grand slam**   **grand prix**
    grand master   **grandstand**   **grand piano**

B   What do these words have in common?

    biff!   **bang!**   **smash!**   **wallop!**

C   How many words can you think of which combine the word **civil** with another word to give new meanings?

D   Use the letters given below to make words horizontally and vertically but not diagonally.

          B   E   E   I   N   O   S   T

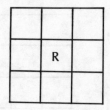

E   What might you just **miss**?

F   Choose the appropriate word.

               charge
    What was the   **price**   of that beautiful watch we saw in the
               cost
    jeweller's shop window?

G   What animals might children keep as **pets**?

A Do you know the meaning of the expressions below?

by the way   **by-product**   **by accident**   **by and by**

B Think of at least three other creatures to fit into each of these six categories.

owl   **dog**   **cat**   **horse**   **cow**   **snake**

C How many meanings can you think of for the word **class**?

D Use the letters given below to make words horizontally and vertically but not diagonally.

A   E   L   N   O   O   P   T

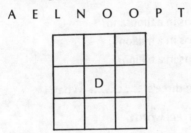

E What is the **thief of time**?

F Which is the correct word?

I'm not sure of his age but, **for** / **on** / **at** a guess, I'd say he was about thirty.

G How do you play **conkers**?

A   Do you know the meaning of these expressions?

crossbar   **cross-country**   **cross-examine**
cross-legged   **cross-purposes**   **crossroads**
cross-section **crossword**

B   What do you **knit** with?
What do you **sew** with?
What do you **embroider** with?

C   How many meanings can you think of for the word **common**?

D   How many zeros in a **thousand**?
How many zeros in a **million**?
How many zeros in a **billion**?

E   **Two's company; three's** .... What?

F   Choose the correct word:
Our eldest son is in the navy, but at present he's at home
for
at   leave.
on

G   **Once upon a time** . . . How does this sentence normally continue?

A   Which word can come before all these to make new words?

grown	board	stop	length	face
scale	house	circle	time	moon

B   Make sentences to show how the following words might be used.

fat   overweight   plump   stout   tubby   obese

C   How many meanings can you think of for **flat**? (Think of music, accommodation, beer and land.)

D   Find the seven capital cities hidden in this text.

I had to call on Donald last week and found the trip a risky one. I went on my horse (I had to climb on, naturally) and had a mad ride along the street charging at hens and cocks, boys and girls regardless. 'Go slow!' I shouted. Was I brave? A hero? Me? Never.

E   **Time and** what **wait for no man**?

F   Which of these words may be used in the following sentences?

refuse   decline   reject

I regret that I must .... your invitation.

The horse .... the apple that Pat had brought for her.

Despite our protests, we were .... permission to film the event.

The proposals were .... without further discussion.

Do you intend to .... their offer then?

G   In what circumstances in Britain would you pick up a telephone and dial 999?

A   Apart from **French fries**, what other **French** things can you think of? Try food (three times), furniture, and a view of the garden.

B   What do the following sell?

grocer   **greengrocer**   **butcher**
baker   **ironmonger**   **department store**

C   Find the missing word.

They **didn't have the** .... to leave him behind.
She had **set her** .... on a new bicycle.
His .... **is in the right place.**

D   Can you think of a word meaning 'to add flavour' which sounds the same as a word referring to 'part of a year'?

E   Why might you want to **turn a blind eye** to something?

F   How could these words be used in the sentences below?
reach   **arrive**   **get**

When they .... to the airport the plane had already left.
By the time I .... the front of the queue they had almost sold out.
We're not going to .... back home until morning at this rate.
You're due to .... in New York at about eight.
She .... the conclusion that he didn't know what he was talking about.

G   If you were sitting in the cinema behind someone who was making a lot of noise, what noise would you make to ask them to be quiet?

List as many words as you can ending with **-proof**, and write sentences showing how they are used. If you are working in a group, score one point for each word not produced by any other group, plus one more point for each correct sentence.

What areas are referred to as follows?

the Continent	**the Middle East**	**the Far East**
the New World	**the Third World**	**the Commonwealth**

Explain the following expressions.

at crack of dawn   the **crack of doom**   a **fair crack of the whip**

Can you think of a word meaning 'a type of grain' which sounds the same as 'something painful on one's foot'?

Someone who's **broke** hasn't got **two pennies to** .... What?

Which prepositions are needed to complete the sentences below?

Let's raise our glasses and drink .... Gillian and Robert.

The young woman drank .... the professor's words eagerly.

Come on, everybody drink .... It's time to go.

G Can you explain how the following are used?

current account	**deposit account**	**crossed cheque**
cheque card	**cash card**	**Eurocheque card**

32

A Think of as many words as you can beginning with **red**, and write sentences to show how they are used. If you are working in a group, score one point for each word not produced by any other group, plus one more point for each correct sentence.

B A **frog** usually **croaks**. What sounds do the following animals make

owl   dog   cat   horse   cow   snake

C Can you think of three words that are specially connected with **boarding**? (Think of education, holidays and travel.)

D Can you think of a word meaning 'press repeatedly' which sounds like a word meaning 'require'?

E How might you **hit the nail on the head**?

F Choose the appropriate word to complete this sentence.

I'm afraid I shall have to take this skirt back to the shop. It's a bit
	great	
too	**huge**	for me.
	big	

G How old do you think someone needs to be to be called the following?

baby	girl	boy	youth
young man	young woman	middle-aged	
old woman	old man	OAP	

A What might you be **100 metres above**?
What might you eat out of **shells**?
What might you **like to be beside**?
Where might you look for **flotsam and jetsam**?

B 'The music was great but the food was ....' Find some
words to express your displeasure.

C Can you think of any sayings which include the word **grave**?

D Can you think of a place on the Mediterranean which sounds the
same as an oily substance?

E How many expressions can you think of using the word **eye**?

F Choose the correct word to complete this sentence.
Doctors are now firmly convinced that cigarettes are bad
on
for your health.
to

G How might you address the following people or groups in a formal
situation?

the **audience**   an **ambassador**   a **prince**   a **princess**
a **president**   a **prime minister**

34

A Find as many words as you can that end in -**ish**, and write sentences showing how they are used. If you are working in a group, score one point for each word not produced by any other group, plus one more point for each correct sentence.

B How are the words below used?

quarrel	**squabble**	**argue**
bicker	**fall out**	**disagree**

C He **has a** .... **with** children.

She always **gets her own** ....

I want to **pay my** ....

You'd better **mend your** ....**s** .

He's very **set in his** ....

D Can you think of a word referring to 'part of a tree' which sounds like a word meaning 'to incline the head'?

E How do you **break the ice** at parties?

F Choose the correct word to complete the sentence:

Mrs Evans is **with** / **at** / **on** the phone at the moment. Would you like to take a seat?

G How many towns in Britain can you find beginning with C, L and E? e.g. Cardiff, London and Edinburgh.

If we can buy **second-hand** gloves, does this mean that we can buy **second-foot** shoes? What other words can you find beginning with **second-**?

Which is the odd one out in each of the following sets of words?

London	aluminium	beech	cod	beef
Glasgow	copper	birch	trout	liver
Hull	carbon	oak	haddock	pork
Exeter	tin	yew	plaice	lamb

He isn't .... in the head.

She's .... as rain.

.... enough.

.... you are.

.... oh!

Quite ....

Can you think of a word meaning 'correct' which sounds like a word referring to 'a means of communication'?

A stitch in time saves ... three.

Is this a good enough return on your investment?

Which of the words below would you use in the following sentences?

reason   pretext   excuse

George just couldn't stand the office any more so he left early on the .... that his daughter was sick.

She said she was going to take the dog for a walk, but perhaps that was simply her .... to go to the pub.

Ann was better qualified than the other candidates and that's the .... why she got the job.

G   Can you complete the following quotation from Muhammad Ali, the boxer?

Float like a .... , sting like a ....

A   Think of as many words as you can beginning with **over-**, and write sentences showing how they are used. If you are working in a group, score one point for each word not produced by any other group, plus one more point for each correct sentence.

B   What are the functions of the following?

     solicitor   **barrister**   **juror**   **magistrate**   **judge**

C   How many meanings can you find for the noun **match**?

D   Can you think of a word meaning 'a light colour' which sounds the same as a word referring to 'a container'?

E   **Too many cooks** .... What?

F   Which of the words below would you use in the following sentences?

     bath   **bathe**

     Mike and Andi normally take turns to .... the baby.

     He usually .... before he shaves but today was an exception.

     That's a nasty cut. You'd better let me .... it with something.

     If the sea's still warm enough at four o'clock we'll .... then.

     When the sun rises it .... the mountains with gold.

G   Someone across the street from you is walking past a building site. You suddenly notice that a workman has dropped a hammer which looks as though it might hit the person on the head. How would you call out a warning?

A   Think of as many words as you can beginning with **under-** and write sentences showing how they are used. If you are working in a group, score one point for each word not produced by any other group, plus one more point for each correct sentence.

B   List the kinds of **weather** you do and do not like.

C   How many meanings can you find for **pitch**?

D   Can you think of one word which can mean both 'design' and 'the top of a hill'?

E   What might you say **off the record**? Does it have anything to do with LPs or the Olympics?

F   Choose the correct word to complete the sentence:

                              at

Charlotte takes a delight **for** teasing her little brother.

                              in

G   What are these places famous for?

Stratford-upon-Avon   **Stonehenge**

Wimbledon   **Hadrian's Wall**

A What are the differences between the following pairs of words?

official/officious   **continual/continuous**

exceptional/exceptionable   **respectful/respectable**

B Make a list of all the **cutlery, crockery** and other **equipment** you might find in a kitchen.

C How many **points** can you think of?

D Can you think of a word which can mean 'container' and also refer to 'a part of the human body'?

E What might you **spend money like**?

What might **news spread like**?

F Choose the correct word to complete the sentence:

I know there's something strange going on, but I just can't put

my   **thumb**
     finger   on it at the moment.
     hand

G Can you distinguish between these words?

city	town	village	hamlet
district	ward	suburb	quarter

A Which of these words is different from the others and why?

incapable   **inseparable**   **inflammable**   **inhuman**

B Can you label ten more parts of this face?

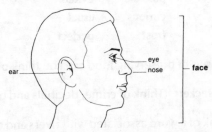

C Which word would complete the following dialogue?

I've **done** .... **out of** this investment. You'd **do** .... **to** follow my example.

That **may** .... **be**, but I'm .... **and truly** broke.

Oh .... , perhaps it's **just as** ....

.... , what a thing to say!

D Can you think of a word for a long structure which is also the name of an indoor game?

E What **stands to reason**?

F Choose the appropriate word:

Mark is a very timid boy. He couldn't say boo to a   **goose**
                                                     duck.
                                                     hen

G '........................ . That is the question.'

What is the question?

A Find the correct beginning to make each word on the right negative.

mis-	able	take
un-	possible	evitable
im-	curious	usual
in-	trust	perfect

B How many ways of preserving food can you think of?

C Name three **rackets**. (Think of crime, decibels and balls.)

D Can you think of a word associated with rivers and canals which reminds us of money?

E When might we all be **in the same boat**?
It's **not the same** without Mabel. What isn't?
What is the **same old story**?
What is the **same again, please**?

F Which of the following combinations would you use in the sentences below?

agree to   agree on   agree with

Can I take it that we're all agreed .... this point at least?

He was reluctant at first but he finally agreed .... it.

You look wonderful. The Mediterranean climate obviously agrees .... you.

Do you all agree .... what I suggest?

G Name the signs of the zodiac. Do you know yours?

A   Give the plural of the following words:
thief   sister-in-law   tomato   medium   wolf

B   If you exploded with laughter, would you **titter, giggle, guffaw, chuckle** or **snigger**?

C   What must you **move with** so as not to be old-fashioned?

What must you **move** when you're doing your utmost to get something done?

What have you **moved** when you've got a new address?

D   Can you think of a word referring to someone who has invited you for dinner which also means a large number?

E   Do you have to be in a car to **take turns**?

F   How would you use the following verbs in the sentences below?
play at   play with   play down   play on   play off

The appeal played .... the public's love of animals.

What do you think you're playing .... ? You'll break my machine if you use it like that.

He craftily played one friend .... against the other for his own purposes.

She didn't want to make a fuss so she played .... the incident.

Carol is playing .... the idea of emigrating.

G   What are the **mass media**?
What is a **press box**?
What is the **gutter press**?

42

A   Think of as many words as you can beginning with **book**, and write
     sentences showing how they are used. If you are working in a
     group, score one point for each word not produced by any other
     group plus one more point for each correct sentence.

B   If left is **port**, what is right? Is it **fore, aft** or **starboard**?

C   What might be **all over the shop**?
     Why might we **shut up shop**?
     When might we **talk shop**?
     When might someone **shop** us?

D   Can you think of a word for a nocturnal animal which also has a
     connection with outdoor games?

E   **Well, I'll be. . . . . !** What will you be?

F   Write sentences showing three pairs of opposites using these
     words.

     high   long   tall   low   short

G   What have the following in common?

     Granada   Yorkshire   HTV
     Border   Anglia   Thames

A in____ble im____ble

Find words to fit this pattern with the following meanings:

impossible to do; impossible to believe; faultless; impossible to rub out; never changing; lacking ability.

Can you find any more?

B How many words and expressions can you think of connected with **banking**?

C Would you normally **make the best of a bad** .... , or **give it up as a bad** .... ? (You shouldn't **have much of a** .... filling in these gaps.)

D Can you think of one word which means both a foundation and a military installation?

E **There are no flies on** Jane. Does this mean she sprays herself regularly?

F Choose the correct word.

The donkey is used in many parts of the world as a

beast of
carriage.
burden.
load.
weight.

G What do you know about these days?

St George's Day   St Patrick's Day   St Andrew's Day

St Valentine's Day   Guy Fawkes' Night

44

A Explain these terms.

checkup **checkout** **checklist** **checkmate**

B Match the pairs in sentences.

win	**opponent**
defeat	**reward**
gain	**race**
beat	**enemies**
earn	**admission**

C What verb is missing from the following sentences?

It was too difficult – I just couldn't .... it all ....
Could you .... the dress .... an inch?
She earns extra money by .... paying guests.
The confidence trickster .... everybody ....

D Can you think of a word which refers to a kind of competition and also puts people into categories?

E If I'm **beside myself**, am I a twin?

F What's wrong with this sentence?

I wanted to be sure the letter arrived in time for Christmas, so I made sure it went airpost.

G **You .... fool!** How can you fill the gap?

A   Think of as many words as you can ending in **-ify**, and write sentences showing how they are used. If you are working in a group, score one point for each word not produced by any other group, plus one more for each correct sentence.

B   How many words can you think of for the act of eating?
e.g. **nibble** and **chew**

C   What noun is missing from the following sentences?

This is the .... that Jack built.

The .... rose at eleven thirty.

People who live in glass .... shouldn't throw stones.

A dog needs to be .... trained.

Some people are tremendously .... proud.

D   Can you think of a word for a flower which also means 'got up'?

E   **You can't take it with you**. What? Where?

F   Which of the words below would you use in the following sentences?

easy   simple

The home team won a(n) .... victory over their opponents.

Her voice is very .... on the ear.

The .... fact is that we can't afford a new car.

It was just a very .... cottage but beautifully furnished.

G   What do you understand by the following?

trunk call   **reverse charge**   **IDD**

directory enquiries   **answering machine**

A Label this diagram with the following
parts of the body:

shoulder   **elbow**
knee   **shin**
wrist   **thigh**
ankle   **heel**

B What are your favourite **hobbies**?

C What kinds of things do we do **by ear, by heart, by word of mouth**
and **by hand**?

D Can you think of a word meaning 'large' which sounds the same as
one meaning 'to make a sharp, unpleasant sound'?

E Who is more likely to tell you to **use more elbow grease**, your
doctor or your boss? Why?

F Match the pairs:

a **slice** of	**paper**
a **puff** of	**bread**
a **drop** of	**salt**
a **piece** of	**rope**
a **lump** of	**ham**
a **length** of	**smoke**
a **hunk** of	**sugar**
a **pinch** of	**oil**

G What do you understand by the following?

Greenwich Mean Time	**British Summer Time**	**time zones**
Eastern Standard Time	**European Time**	

A   Name the parts of a book: first the physical parts, then the contents.

B   **Candidate** and **constituency** are two terms connected with politics. Think of as many others as you can in three minutes.

C   Find the missing word.

You're .... **your rocker**.

Sorry, sir, the steak and kidney pie is ....

He's a bit .... **colour** today.

This fish is going ....

And **they're** .... !

.... **you go** then.

D   Can you think of a word meaning 'give the impression' which sounds like one meaning 'a line of stitches'?

E   What do some people **work their fingers to**? And what do they **keep their nose to**?

F   Match the pairs:

a **herd** of	ants
a **flock** of	fish
a **pack** of	cattle
a **swarm** of	sheep
an **army** of	wolves
a **shoal** of	bees

G   Is **Hell** a bad place? Is **hell** a bad word?

A Think of as many words as you can ending in **-ic**, and write sentences showing how they are used. If you are working in a group, score one point for each word not produced by any other group, plus one more point for each correct sentence.

B Fill in the extremes.

························

not very good.

The play was **all right.**

quite good.

························

C Find the missing word.

He's a bit of a ············off really.

Let's have a ············ **of hands.**

He wants to go into ············ **business.**

Penelope enjoys ············ **jumping.**

D Can you think of a word for 'remaining' which also means 'not right'?

E I may **have a pain** in any part of my body, but what might I **be a pain** in?

F How are the following prepositions used in the sentences below?

in   at   on

They'll probably arrive ············ the weekend.

I hope it snows ············ Christmas Day.

The postman normally comes ············ lunchtime.

You can expect reasonably warm weather ············ the spring.

Carol is doing postgraduate research ············ Cambridge now.

We've found a nice little flat ············ Cambridge.

G What do the following terms have in common?

Jubilee   Bakerloo   Circle   Central   Northern

A Explain the following.

pushcart   **pushover**   **push-ups**
push-button   **pushchair**   **push off**

B **genius**   **talent**   **skill**   **ability**
It takes one of these at least to know the difference!

C Oops! I've **put my** ………… **in it** again.
Come on, **put your best** ………… **forward**.
Elizabeth is still ………… **loose and fancy free**.
All very well, but who's going to ………… **the bill**?

D Give two letters which sound like an Indian tent.

E If I **haven't got a leg to stand on**, do I necessarily need crutches?

F What's the difference between these pairs of sentences?

The old man was killed **by** a heavy wooden beam.
The old man was killed **with** a heavy wooden beam.
She was driven to the station **with** her daughter.
She was driven to the station **by** her daughter.

G Pronounce these and write them in full.
St.   **Rd.**   **Ave.**   **Terr.**   **Boul.**

A   .... **graph**   .... **site**   .... **troops**

.... **mount**   .... **phrase**   .... **phernalia**

What fills the gap and what does each complete word mean?

B   Draw your **family tree**. How many different relationships, such as **aunt** or **niece**, can you fill in?

C   A .... **for your thoughts**.

He keeps **turning up like a bad** ....

It cost me a **pretty** .... , I can tell you.

.... **from Heaven**.

D   A **shoemaker** would use this but **not first**. Find one word to fit both parts of the clue.

E   How would you say the following?

$57 - 34 = 23$ $10 \times 10 = 100$

$60 \div 6 = 10$ $7,435 + 7 = 7,442$

F   Match the pairs.

dog	lamb
cat	cub
elephant	foal
sheep	tadpole
goat	puppy
lion	fawn
frog	kitten
deer	calf
horse	kid

G   What do you understand by the following?

MP   **PM**   **mpg**   **pm**   **PMG**   **mph**

Symbols used in the key

** This symbol means that you can find more information about the words or expressions in the Longman Dictionary of Contemporary English. The number refers to the page you should turn to.

△△ This symbol means that you can find more information about the words or expressions in the Longman Lexicon of Contemporary English. The number refers to the page you should turn to.

A The suffix **-ship** indicates the state of being something. For example, **membership** means the state of being a member of a club or society; **friendship** means the state of being friends or the feeling which holds friends together. It can also indicate the art or skill of certain activities: *fine* **musicianship** or *great* **scholarship**. It may also sometimes mean the whole group of people involved in an activity: *the* **readership** *of a magazine*.

B 1 chisel 2 mallet 3 pliers 4 screwdriver 5 plane
** 1119

C To **pull a fast one** means to deceive someone: e.g. *Thomas discovered the painting was a fake. The dealer had clearly pulled a fast one on him.*
To **pull rank** means to take advantage of your position of authority to make other people do as you want them to: e.g. *It was clearly the boss's job to meet delegates at the airport but she pulled rank on me so I had to do it myself.*
To **pull your weight** means to do your fair share of the work and is usually used in the negative: e.g. *Bob arrives at the office late and leaves early. He simply isn't pulling his weight these days.*
To **pull someone/something to pieces** means to criticize someone or something by pointing out the weak points or faults: e.g. *My plan was pulled to pieces at the meeting.*
To **pull someone's leg** means to make gentle fun of someone: e.g. *She told me I'd won £5,000, but she was just pulling my leg.*

D cold cord word ward warm

E Someone who often drops things they are carrying or trying to catch.

F Humphrey is married **to** my sister Julie.
Married is usually followed by the preposition **to**.

G Time to stop drinking in a pub in most parts of Britain. Public houses are only allowed to open during certain hours. When closing time approaches, the landlord calls **Time (gentlemen) please** or rings a bell, after which clients are allowed to finish their drinks but not to order more.

A Notice particularly words like **international, interview, interdependent, interaction, interlaced, interface, interpolate** – the Latin meaning of **inter-** as 'between' is clear in these examples. But beware of a word like *interest*, where **inter-** is not a prefix: taking **inter-** away leaves you without a full word.
** 547, B8

B

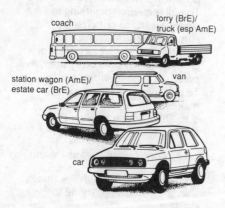

coach

lorry (BrE)/ truck (esp AmE)

station wagon (AmE)/ estate car (BrE)

van

car

C The biggest or most important part of a difficult task is often referred to as **half the battle**: e.g. *When you want a new job, getting an interview is half the battle.*
A **half-baked** idea has not been properly planned or thought about, and therefore will not work in practice.
Flags may fly at the top of a pole or half-way down, at **half-mast**, to show that something sad has happened; that someone important has died, for example. If we **go halves** we share the cost of something, such as the bill in a restaurant.

A **half-hearted** action is one showing little effort and no real interest: e.g. *We made a half-hearted attempt to contact him but we gave up after a few phone calls.*

D

C	A	B
O	N	E
O	D	D

cab (= another word for taxi)
one
odd (= strange or unusual)
coo (= noise made by a pigeon or dove)
and
bed

E **Kick the bucket** is a slang expression for **die**. It is usually used in a humorous way about someone you don't know.

F **Out of order** means broken or broken down: e.g. *The machine is out of order.*
Out of work means unemployed: e.g. *Many people have now been out of work for over a year.*
Out of the question means impossible, not to be considered for a moment: e.g. *We might be able to afford a second-hand car, but buying a new one is out of the question.*

G This comes from the wedding ceremonies of many Christian churches in the UK and the US, in which bride and groom promise to stay together '**for richer for poorer, in sickness or in health, to love and to cherish, till death us do part.**'

A The following nouns can be formed by adding the suffix **-ment** to a verb: **arrangement, attachment, excitement, bewilderment, astonishment, judgement, amusement, replacement** and **wonderment**. There are a number of other words ending in -ment which are not formed in this way, such as **ferment, filament, garment, lineament, medicament, torment**. ** B13

B A **cafe** is a small eating place, which serves hot and cold non-alcoholic drinks and either cakes or snacks such as bacon and eggs or sausages and chips.
A **restaurant** provides a full meal service, and often has a licence to serve alcoholic drinks. Waiters and waitresses serve you at your table. A **restaurant** is somewhere you might **go out** for a meal to; a **cafe** is not.
Finally, a **pub** – short for **public house** – serves beer and other alcoholic drinks as well as soft drinks and snacks. Some pubs serve full meals too.
△△ 231

C A **hard-and-fast rule** is one that cannot or should not be broken or adjusted. For example: *Don't drink and drive!*
An egg should be cooked in boiling water for at least five minutes if it is to be **hard-boiled**. If it is cooked for a short time it will be **soft-boiled**.
Someone who is **hard-boiled** is noted for not showing their feelings, particularly as a result of bitter experiences.
The **hard shoulder** is the strip of road alongside a motorway or main road which you can pull on to if for some reason you have to stop.
A book may be a **hardback**, with hard covers, or a **paperback**, with thin cardboard covers like this one.
You are **hard of hearing** if you have difficulty in hearing.

D One word is **paper**, which provides us with **writing paper** and **paper knife** (a knife used for slitting open envelopes).

E If you persist with an argument for too long or carry out a plan of action to a point where it no longer makes sense, or particularly if you continue with a joke until it is no longer funny, you may be accused of **carrying things too far**: e.g. *My daughter's name is April. We thought about calling her April May June Smith, but decided that would be carrying things too far.*

F Generally speaking, we **do** an action and **make** something which was not there before: e.g. **do** *the washing*, but **make** *a fire*. However, there are many fixed expressions which follow no rules, but simply have to be learnt. The correct expressions here are:
I have to **do** the washing up.
The children were **making** faces . . .
I didn't have time to **make** the bed . . .
Jessica decided to have nothing more to **do** with George.
We're staying late at the office to **do** the accounts.
** 631–3

A **Out** goes in!
** 731

B If you are running hard, you may have to stop to **catch your breath**, that is, to take in some air. If you stay out in the cold night air you may **catch your death** (**of cold**). If someone in authority finds you doing something wrong you may **catch it**, that is, you may be punished or reprimanded. If you **catch somebody out** you take them by surprise or find them doing something they shouldn't be.

C The missing word is **green.**
A **green belt** is a strip of land round a town or city where building is not allowed, so that the countryside remains unspoilt.
A good gardener is said to have **green fingers**.
A **greenhorn**, especially in American English, is a novice.
A **greenhouse** is a structure of glass in which the temperature is higher than in the open air, so that plants which need protection from the cold and the wind can be grown.
A **green light** is, really or metaphorically, a signal to begin an action.

D Another word for rubbish is **waste** and the part of the body which sounds exactly like this word is **waist**.

E The **head** and the **foot** of the stairs are at the top and the bottom respectively. So are the **head** and **foot** of a bed.

F We travel **by** almost any kind of vehicle: **by** bus, **by** train, **by** taxi, **by** car, **by** bicycle (although it is perhaps more common to say 'I went there **on** my bike'.).
However, when we walk we go **on** foot.

G They are all places where students might live while they are studying at a university, polytechnic or college.
A **hostel** is a building in which young people may stay cheaply, often in dormitories or shared rooms.
Youth hostels are similar, except that they are intended for young travellers and tend to be in the countryside.
A **hall of residence** is a building provided and run by a university for its students, usually with comfortably-furnished individual rooms and facilities for communal eating, sports, etc.
Bed-sitter refers to a single room in a block of flats or a large private house converted for the purpose, which serves as both bedroom and living room.
Home is probably the easiest option of all for a student, but not a popular choice in Britain as the tradition has long been to choose a university in a different part of the country from one's home town.

A There are many possibilities. For example **self-assertive** means forceful in making others take notice of oneself, or in claiming things for oneself e.g. *For Heaven's sake, don't let them bully you, try to be more self-assertive.* **Self-conscious** means nervous and uncomfortable about oneself as seen by others e.g. *He could never be an actor; he's too self-conscious.* **Self-denial** means the act or habit of holding oneself back from doing enjoyable things, e.g. *No, thank you, I won't have another piece of cake. I really must practise a little self-denial, otherwise none of my clothes will fit me.* **Self-evident** means plainly true without need of proof, e.g. *It's self-evident that he hasn't a chance of passing the exam, so why is he entering for it?* **Self-possessed** means calm and confident, e.g. *I envy Myra; she never gets ruffled. She'd look self-possessed in the middle of an earthquake.*
** 836–9, B9

B They are the four suits in a pack of playing cards.
△ △ 530

C For example: *Keep your feet on the* **ground** (= the earth beneath you). *What are the* **grounds** (= the evidence, basis) *for your accusations? I'll see you at the* **ground** (= the place where games are played). *Stand your* **ground** (= the territory that you are defending). Notice also the verb 'to **ground**' which has several meanings, including to prevent someone leaving the ground (e.g. a pilot who has misbehaved); and the past tense and participle of **grind** as in **ground** *coffee.*
** 462

D Another word for heaviness is **weight**, which sounds exactly like **wait**.

E **Hold your tongue!** is a rude way of telling someone to stop talking when the listener is annoyed by what they are saying.

F What is the reason **for** his disgrace?
The preposition **for** is used after **reason** before another noun or a verb in the *-ing* form: *What is your reason* **for** *lying to me?* The preposition **to** is used after **reason** before a verb in the infinitive: *You may be angry, but there's no reason* **to** *scream and shout.*

G You are probably lying almost unconscious in the boxing ring. You are **out for the count** if after being knocked down you are unable to get up and be ready to box again within ten seconds.

A Notice words like **subcommittee, subconscious, subdivide, submarine, submerge, subplot** and **subsidiary**, where the prefix **sub-** gives the sense of 'under' or 'less important'. Notice also words like *substance*, where the **sub-** element has lost any original meaning it might have had.
** 1053–6, B9

B In Britain the ministers of the government and the leading members of the opposition sit on the **front benches** of the House of Commons, and are often referred to as **frontbenchers**.
A soldier is said to be in the **front line** in a war if he or she is in the area where most of the fighting is taking place.
The **front page** of a newspaper is where the most newsworthy items go, so the **front page** would be held, that is, not completed, if some important news was anticipated.
The **front-runner** is the person who has the best chance of success in competing for something, such as a job or position in government.

C I saw a man jump;
Over a house I saw the moon;
Beneath the sea I saw a fish;
Driving a car I saw the Queen;
Upon a bike I saw a girl;

Within a glass (= a mirror) I saw the one who saw all this (myself!)

D You would be wasting time or effort by returning to a subject or argument which has already been settled. However much you **flog a dead horse**, it is not going to get up and walk!

E There are three possible combinations:

I'm determined to
call a halt
put a stop
put an end
to this silliness.

F **Ready, steady, go!** is often said at the beginning of a race. **Red, amber, green** is the sequence followed by a set of traffic lights. **Every Tom, Dick and Harry** means everybody, while **lock, stock and barrel** means completely.

G The **best man** at a traditional Christian wedding in the UK and the USA is the person chosen by the bridegroom to accompany him during the ceremony and help him at the reception which usually follows. The best man looks after the wedding ring until the bridegroom has to place it on the bride's finger. At the reception he often reads out greetings messages and is asked to give a short and often humorous speech.

A A **short circuit** is a faulty electrical connection that makes the current flow along the wrong path. This can cause power breakdowns, and even fires.
A **shortfall** occurs when an amount, for example a company's profits, is lower than had been expected or hoped for.
Shortbread is not bread at all, but a biscuit made of flour, butter, and sugar.
A **shortcoming** is a weakness or defect in something or someone.
If you are on a **short list**, you are on a list of candidates for a job or prize who have been chosen as the most suitable out of a much longer list of original applicants.
A person, for example a secretary, who knows **shorthand**, uses special symbols to take notes rapidly. The **shorthand** notes can be typed up in full later.

B Here are a few possibilities: **short story, novel, biography, autobiography, essay, play, drama, prose, poetry, verse,** and **sonnet.**
△ △ G349–51

C Someone who is **like a fish out of water** is uncomfortable because they are in a strange place or situation: e.g. *I'd never been to a formal dinner party before, and felt like a fish out of water for the first half hour.*
To **have other fish to fry** is to have other, probably more important, affairs to attend to: e.g. *They asked me to stay behind to watch the balloon blowing contest, but I had other fish to fry and left as soon as I could.*
If someone is **fishing for compliments** they are trying to make someone say something admiring: e.g. *I've just had my fortieth birthday. Do you think I LOOK forty, Jane?*
If something **sounds or smells fishy** it makes one doubtful or suspicious: e.g. *Did you believe what he said? His story sounded a bit fishy to me.*

D John must be either an ordained priest who is allowed to conduct a marriage ceremony, or a registrar who is allowed to conduct civil marriages, that is, those which are not conducted in a place of worship. The word **marry** means both to be legally united with someone of the opposite sex, and to perform the ceremony of marriage.
** 642

E If you're making a great effort to do something you are **putting your back into** the job.

F **Congratulations** is usually followed by **on**, so: Congratulations **on** winning the scholarship.

G The train on which you were travelling would stop suddenly. The **communication cord** in a train is a chain which you can pull in an emergency to stop the train. If you pulled it at any other time you might have to pay a fine.
** 201

A A **double bass** is a large stringed instrument which makes a very deep (= bass) sound, and which is frequently used in classical and jazz music.

A **double bed** is a bed for two people. When booking a hotel room for two, you will be asked whether you want a double or a twin (= two single beds.)

A bus with two floors, like the typical London bus, is called a **double-decker**.

A **doubles** game is a game, usually of tennis, between two couples. We speak about **women's** or **men's doubles**, and **mixed doubles**. Something which is **double-edged** has two meanings or purposes, and, like a sword, may be dangerous. So a **double-edged** remark may seem amiable, but probably hides a more unpleasant intention.

In cold climates, or noisy areas, for example, close to an airport, it is common to have **double-glazing**: a window is provided with two sheets of glass (or glass substitute), and the thin layer of air between the two keeps out the cold and noise.

B Some possible pairs of opposites are: **new/old; young/old; new/full; modern/ancient; modern/old-fashioned; modern/antique**. Generally speaking **new** refers to something that exists now but has been in existence for only a short time. Its usual opposite is **old**. When referring to people, however, the opposite of **old** is **young**. Note that the opposite of a **new** moon is a **full** moon. **Modern** may be used of both people and things, and means belonging to the present time. Its opposite may be **old-fashioned**, **antique** or **ancient**: e.g. *an old-fashioned person/an old-fashioned dress/an antique chair/a modern chair/an ancient monument/a modern skyscraper* △△ 586–9

C The missing word is **world**. **On top of the world** means very happy. To **think the world of** someone is to be extremely fond of them. **Out of this world** means absolutely wonderful, and **what/who/where** etc **in the world** is a way of expressing surprise.

D fish   fist   fiat   feat   meat
A **fiat** is a command by someone in a position of power: e.g. *The changes were brought about by presidential fiat.*

E They are not real tears at all; crocodiles are said to pretend to be sad to attract their victims. So you weep **crocodile tears** when you are only pretending to find something unfortunate.

F The noun **discussion** is followed by **about** or **on**, but the verb **discuss** is not followed by any particle, so:
We had a discussion about students' grants.
We discussed students' grants.

G **A, B, C, D, E, F** and **G**. Compare the names for the notes in the **tonic solfa: doh, re, mi, fa, so, la, ti.** △△ 510

A **cold-blooded** action is one showing a complete lack of feeling: e.g. *a cold-blooded murder*.

A **cold-hearted** person or action lacks all human kindness and sympathy: e.g. *his cold-hearted rejection of his children*.

If you have **cold feet** about something, you have doubts and anxieties that prevent you from proceeding with it: e.g. *They were going to be married in June, but she got cold feet and broke off the engagement at the last minute*.

You might **give the cold shoulder** to someone you do not want to meet, who has perhaps upset you in some way; you take no notice of them and ignore any attempts at social contact which they may make: e.g. *After their argument John gave her the cold shoulder*.

B Some possibilities are: **white, silver, grey, black, brown, hazel, russet, tan, chocolate, bronze, khaki, red, scarlet, vermilion, carmine, crimson, pink, maroon, magenta, green, olive, yellow, gold, purple, indigo, violet, lavender, mauve, blue** and **orange**. The primary colours are **red, blue** and **yellow**. The seven colours of the rainbow are **red, orange, yellow, green, blue, indigo** and **violet**.
△ △ 552–3

C The missing word is **nothing**.
Think nothing of it is a way of responding to thanks, similar in meaning to 'It was a pleasure'.
It cost **next to nothing** is a way of saying something was extremely cheap.
There's nothing for it means there is no alternative to the action proposed: e.g. *We've got no money left for a taxi, so there's nothing for it — we'll have to walk home*.

I'll do **nothing of the kind** is an indignant refusal to do whatever has been suggested; e.g. *'I suggest you apologise to Mr Worthington.' 'I'll do nothing of the kind!'*

That's nothing to do with me means I'm not responsible for that.

You ain't nothing but a hound dog is the title of a song by Elvis Presley.

D **gold   hold   held   hell   bell**

E 'Never look a **gift horse** in the mouth.' Do not, in other words, seek to criticize what someone else gives you or does for you. (One way of checking a horse's quality and condition is to examine its mouth.)

F To **dress** and to **get dressed** mean simply to put clothes on: e.g. *She dressed quickly and came downstairs*. But for some social groups **dress** has the special meaning of 'put on evening clothes': e.g. *They always dress for dinner*. The verb **dress in** draws attention to the clothes one is wearing: e.g. *He dresses in all the latest fashions.|The beggar was dressed in rags*.
To **dress up** is to put on fancy dress, a costume or a disguise of some kind. But note the expression **dressed up to the nines**, which means dressed in one's best and showiest clothes.

G It is **April Fools' Day (All Fools' Day)** when, up to midday, it is common for people to play practical jokes on each other.

A There are many possibilities. For example, a **highbrow** is someone with very learned or cultured tastes; **high-class** means of good quality; **high-flown** means important-sounding but without deep meaning; **high-handed** means arrogant in one's dealings with others, **high life** refers to rich people's life of entertainment and enjoyment; **high-minded** means having very high moral standards; a **high-pitched** voice or sound is very high, not low or deep; **high-powered** means capable of powerful performance; **high-priced** means expensive, often unduly expensive; **high-quality** means of the best kind; a **high-rise** block is a building with many floors containing individual flats; **high-speed** means capable of working or travelling very fast; **high-spirited** means cheerful and lively; and a **high-tension** cable is one which carries a powerful and dangerous electric current.
** 493–5

B **Arson** is the crime of setting fire to property.
Theft is the crime of taking someone else's property from a place.
Burglary is the crime of entering a building (especially a home) by force with the intention of stealing.
Fraud is deceitful behaviour for the purpose of making money which is punishable by law.
Embezzlement is stealing money which is placed in one's care. For example a bank clerk might embezzle money from the bank where he or she works.

Treason is the crime of disloyalty to one's country, especially by helping its enemies or by violent opposition to those in power.
△△ 134–136

C One word that fits is **word**.
To **keep your word** is not to break a promise.
To **break your word** means exactly the opposite.
To **eat your words** means to admit that you've said something wrong
To **take someone at their word** is to act on the belief that they mean what they say: e.g. *George and Mildred said to come round any time so we took them at their word and called on them one evening.*
To **be as good as one's word** is to keep one's promise.

D **Smiles.** (There is a **mile** between the first and last letters – sorry!)

E No! I am simply thinking of a different set of problems. 'This is **a fine kettle of fish**' means 'We certainly have some problems here!'
** 573

F The correct collocations are:
When she realized she had to return the money she decided to **pay up** at once.
If you wish, we can **pay** the money straight **into** your account.
If you supply the food, I'll **pay for** the drinks.
His work was terrible, so after a week we decided to **pay** him **off**.

G When someone is brought to court for some offence and has no permanent address, he or she is said to be of **no fixed abode**.
** 2

A The missing word is **for**.
If you **give** someone **what for** you punish them severely.
To **be for it** is to be in trouble with some authority – your parents, for example.
There's gratitude for you is a sarcastic way of saying that someone is being UNgrateful.
If it weren't for someone or something means that without their help (or interference) something good (or annoying) would not have happened.
** 400–1

B With **pond** you can group words for larger and smaller areas of water which is not flowing, e.g. **puddle, pool, loch, lake, lagoon, reservoir, sea**, and **ocean**. With **stream** group words for flowing water, e.g. **brook, burn, river, canal**, and perhaps **tributary, estuary**.
△ △ 564–7

C The word is **time**.
To **kill time** or to **pass the time** is to make time pass quickly by finding something to do: e.g. *We played cards to kill time/to pass the time*.
To **do time** is a slang expression meaning to be in prison: e.g.

He's doing time for burglary.
To **spend time** is to be occupied: e.g. *She spends a lot of her time writing*.
To **waste time** is to use it wrongly: e.g. *Get on with your work and stop wasting time fooling about!*
** 1111–3

D The sound of the letters – 'I owe you' – gives the meaning; an IOU is a note showing your debt to someone usually followed by the sum owed: e.g. *IOU £50*.
** 557

E On the contrary. If you are **full of beans** you are feeling energetic and lively.

F The verb **explain** cannot be used with two objects. We can only **explain** something **to** someone. The noun **explanation** takes the preposition **of**. Thus the two acceptable forms are:
I tried to **explain** the meaning of the phrase **to them**.
What **explanation of** this can you offer?

G The **United Kingdom** (the **UK**) includes **Great Britain** (England, Scotland and Wales) and Northern Ireland.
** 1147

A The suffix **-logy** or **-ology** is used to form the name of a branch of science: e.g. **biology, geology, physiology, meteorology** and **criminology**. (An **anthology** is a collection of writings – usually poems – from different sources.)
** B13

B These are all concerned with the supernatural.
A **witch** is a woman with magical powers, usually used for evil purposes.
A **wizard** is a man with magical powers.
Fairies are small figures with magical powers and human (usually female) form, which often have wings and can fly: they are generally good creatures, although there is a 'wicked fairy' in some stories.
Gnomes, dwarves and **goblins** are all small imaginary figures: **goblins** are ugly, usually unkind or evil and play tricks on people; **dwarves** are small men, such as those who appear in 'Snow White and the Seven Dwarves'; **gnomes** are little old men who live underground and often guard treasure.
All these creatures occur frequently in fairy stories and folk tales, and there are many variations: for example, look up **leprechaun** ** 599.
△△ 168

C The missing word is **sick**.
You **make me sick** if you annoy me.
I'm **sick and tired** of something which I have had enough of,

which I find extremely irritating. If I'm **worried sick** about someone or something, I'm very worried indeed.
** 974

D A typewriter and a prison both have **keys**.
A tree and an elephant both have a **trunk**.
A book and a knight both have a **title** (and possibly **pages**).
A bicycle and an organ both have **pedals**.

E To **give** someone **a piece of your mind** means to tell them angrily and plainly that you do not approve of their behaviour.

F She's very good **at** tennis.
When **good** is used to refer to a particular skill or talent, it is followed by **at**. When we are talking about human relationships, however, **good** can be followed by **with**: e.g. *He's very good* with *children*. When we are referring to specific situations **good** may be used with **in**: e.g. *She's very good* in *a crisis*.

G You might want to include classrooms, teaching blocks, staff accommodation, student hostels or halls of residence, libraries, language laboratories, tennis courts, squash courts, a gymnasium, a swimming pool, laboratories, administration block, shops, bookshops, banks, restaurants or canteens, and bars. Not all universities, of course, have all of these.

Here are some possibilities: A **misfit** is someone who is unsuited to the way they live or the people they live or work with. To **misbehave** is to behave badly. A **misapprehension** is a wrong understanding. So the prefix **mis-** adds the sense of 'wrong' or 'badly' to the main word, or indicates the complete absence or opposite of something as in **mistrust**. (Not all words starting with **mis-** are examples of this prefix: **missing**, for example, does not mean to ruin a song!)
** 663–6, B8

3 **Tell**, which is nearly always transitive, means to communicate something in words to someone else. It can take one object, and is often followed by an indirect object such as **me**, **us**, **her friends**.
Say, which is also usually transitive, functions differently. It must usually have as its object the words that are spoken and may or may not be followed by an indirect object after **to**.
Speak, which is usually intransitive, refers to the act of expressing one's thoughts in words rather than to what is actually said. We might, for example, find this anticlimax to a story:

X: *The dying man spoke in a whisper.*
Y: *Well, what did he say to you?*
X: *He said, 'Farewell, my friends.'*
Y: *What else did he say?*
X: *He told me never to tell anyone – so I won't.*
** 930, △△ 315–6

C **Iron.**
An **iron fist in a velvet glove** means a very firm intention hidden behind a gentle appearance.
If we **strike while the iron is hot**, we do something at the most favourable time.
A very firm leader, such as a severe director of a company or a very strict teacher, might be said to **rule with a rod of iron**.
The **Iron Curtain** is the common name for the border between the countries of the Communist bloc and the rest of the world — a border which is not easy to cross.
** 557–8

D The word is **fine**, which means 'beautiful and of high quality', as in *a fine picture / building / piece of music*, and also 'an amount of money paid as a punishment': e.g. *a parking fine.*

E Because it would mean you had got yourself into trouble through some piece of misbehaviour.
** 507

F She spoke to the crowd **in** a loud voice.
When we talk about the way someone speaks, we often use the preposition **in**: e.g. *He spoke in a whisper.*/*She spoke in riddles.*
But note: *My colleagues and I speak with one voice.*

G **Bye-bye** (or simply **bye**) is a familiar form for **goodbye**. You would say it in informal situations to people you knew well. *Bye-bye, Your Majesty* is definitely not recommended!
△△ 379

A The suffix **-ation** shows the act or action or result of a verb. Thus, for example, **affixation** is the act of attaching an affix to a word. **Conversation** is the act of conversing. A **combination** is what you get when several things are combined. Notice that a number of words ending in **-ation** come from main verbs ending in **-ate**, e.g. **culmination** from **culminate**, **indication** from **indicate**. Some verbs include a further change, e.g. **multiply** gives **multiplication**. Such **complications** can lead to considerable frustration!
** B10

B You **see** anything that happens to be within your sight, whether you intend to or not. You **look** at something quite deliberately. You **watch** something – often an activity – by keeping your eyes fixed on it. Thus:

The sentry looked quickly at his orders, then carried on watching to the front and to his left. But it was dark and he saw nothing. Suddenly . . .
** 945

C If someone is **up to** something, they are doing something naughty or deceitful.
You don't **feel up to** something if you're too tired or not clever or well enough to do something.

What's up? means 'What's the matter?'; **something's up** means something bad or unwelcome is happening.
For these special uses of **up** you cannot use **down** as an opposite.
** 1159

D You can suggest your own answers to this one.

E Either I'm very angry or I'm very hot. In either case, what the question **boils down to** is that a cup of tea might or might not help.
** 104–5

F **Close** may be used with **window**, **meeting** and **conversation**.
Shut may be used with **window**.
End may be used with **meeting**, **conversation** and **relationship**.
So the possibilities are:

Ms Brown
closed/ended the conversation . . .
closed/ended the meeting . . .
closed/shut the window . . .
ended the relationship . . .

G A bylaw is a regulation made by a local body such as a council or railway, which covers minor local matters such as walking on the grass in a park, rather than matters of more general importance, such as wearing a seat-belt in a car, which are covered by the national government.

The suffix **-ism** can indicate a set of ideas or principles, often but not necessarily following the teaching of a prophet or leader: **Buddhism, Marxism, Fascism, feminism, consumerism**. You can even talk about an **ism**, meaning such a set of ideas. (There is no such word, however, as **'wasm'** meaning a past or outdated belief!)
** B12

B You can **open** and **close** things such as doors and windows. You can **turn on** and **turn off** a tap. You can **switch on** and **switch off** or **turn on** and **turn off** a light or other electrical equipment.

C An **open-and-shut** case is a criminal investigation (or other problem) that is easy to settle. The **open season** is the time of year when certain animals or fish may be lawfully killed for sport. An **open house** is one whose owners invite their friends to drop in at any time: many people keep **open house** on Christmas Day, for example, so that friends can call in for a drink and an exchange of seasonal greetings. An **open door policy** is one which allows traders from all countries to trade freely in a particular country. The **open air** is outdoors: for example, you may have an *open-air theatre*. An **open secret** is something

supposed to be a secret, but that everybody knows about. And an **open question** is a question or matter of discussion which has not been resolved, so that a variety of answers or solutions is possible.

D The word is **corporal**, which means 'physical', as in **corporal punishment**, and is also a rank in the British army indicated by two stripes worn on the sleeve.

E No. People who know their business or have knowledge which is based on experience can be said to **know** their **onions**.

F The expression **in love** is followed by **with**, and **fond** is followed by **of**, thus:

Adrian may not be in love **with** Julie, but he's certainly very fond **of** her.

G The **stalls** are seats on the ground floor and usually near the stage. The **gallery** is an upper floor high up at the back of the theatre. The **circle** or **balcony** is an upper floor between the gallery and the stalls. A **box** is a small, more private space with seats, separate from the main seating area, at the side of the theatre and close to the stage. It will not surprise you to know that the ticket price for these different seats varies a good deal.
** 1099

A Like the prefixes **il-, im-** and **ir-, in-** generally indicates 'not', the same as **non-** or **un-**. It is a very common prefix. Once again, not all words beginning with **in-** are examples of this prefix: note, for instance, **interest, insure** and **invite**; and **insect** is not the opposite of **sect**!
** B8

B I **glimpse** something which I have a quick, uncomplete view of.
I **view** something which I examine or look at thoroughly.
To **notice** something is to pay attention to it with the eyes, other senses, or the mind.
To **stare at** something is to look at it steadily for a long time, for example in surprise or shock.
When I **glare at** something I look at it in an annoyed or angry way.
To **catch sight of** something is to notice it for a moment, perhaps because it is moving or hidden. It is, of course, rude to stare!
△△ 289–91

C If I **keep** my **fingers crossed**, I hope for good luck (I might also superstitiously touch wood).
Not only a cook may have **a finger in every pie**, but anyone who takes a part or an interest in everything that's going on.
If I'm working extremely hard, I am **working** my **fingers to the bone**.
Don't **lay a finger on** him means

don't harm him or even touch him in the slightest way.
You can **burn** your **fingers** or **get your fingers burned** if you take a risk or interfere with something that is none of your business and get hurt as a result.
I **twist someone round** my **little finger** when I use charm to get them to do whatever I want.
I have the facts **at** my **fingertips** if all the facts are readily available.
Someone who is **all fingers and thumbs** is immensely clumsy with his or her hands.
** 382

D The first keeps its s**ecret e**ver so well.
In the second you'll find an an**imal ta**med.
You needn't f**eel ba**dly about the third.
(All three are islands in the Mediterranean.)

E 'An apple a day keeps the doctor away,' according to a proverb which predates the health food craze of recent years.

F To **take pity** is followed by **on**, so:
His loss was so great that even his enemies **took pity on** him.

G Sweets of different kinds, chocolates, ice-creams, soft drinks, maybe cakes. In Britain, as in most countries, you will often also find newspapers, comics, cigarettes and so on.

A **Re-** is a common prefix implying **again**, and when it is a prefix with this sense it is pronounced /riː/. For example, **reline**, means to put a new inside covering into; **remarry** means to marry again; to **remodel** is to change the shape of; to **reopen** is to open or begin again; and to **repay** means to pay back.
There are also other words beginning with **re-** in which it is pronounced /rɪ/ or /re/. For example, **remote** means distant in space or time; a **reliable** person or thing may be trusted; something **relevant** is directly connected with the subject being discussed.
** B9

B The first four words are used for objects which have a small distance between opposite surfaces.
Thin is the general word for people and things: e.g. *a thin pencil/dress/shelf*.
Slim and **slender** are both used to describe people who are attractively thin: e.g. *a slim young lad/a slender waist*. **Slender** can also be used for things which are long and thin, as can **fine**, which is often used with threads and materials such as silk, cotton, hair and wire.
Narrow is generally related to things or places which you cannot easily get through or along e.g. *a narrow gate/path*. It may also be used figuratively, to mean limited (*a narrow mind*) or nearly unsuccessful (*a narrow escape*).
** 1102–3, △△ 56–7, 763–4

C The word is **end**.

No **end of** means a lot of, an endless amount of.
Someone **at a loose end** can think of nothing to do.
The **weekend** is, of course, Saturday and Sunday, though you may be able to take an extra day off and get away for **a long weekend**.
The **deep end** is what you would expect it to be in a swimming pool, though someone who **goes off the deep end** is losing his or her temper.
This is the end is an expression of disapproval and a warning of discomforts to come!
And I **get the wrong end of the stick** when I misunderstand the situation. (Sorry. This is **no end of** a long explanation!)

D The first would seem to **be a R**ussian one.
I **came** late to find the second.
With the third we must **stop, I g**ather.

E Not necessarily. To **get all shirty** is to get bad-tempered, angry and rude.

F If you wear those socks you'll catch a cold; they're **damp**.
Kate took a bite of the rich, **moist** Christmas cake.
At this time of year, the jungle is particularly hot and **humid**.
Damp is often used in a bad sense.
Moist is used particularly of food and parts of the body, and often has a good sense.
Humid is usually used of climate or weather.

G Hockey, or polo.
** 498, ** 798

A **Pre-** usually indicates 'before, in front of, in advance,' in terms of either time or place or status, e.g. **preordained, preeminent, prerequisite**. The most obvious example is **prefix**: but perhaps we shouldn't **preempt** your choice of words!

B All the words refer in some way or other to **work**, which has the most general meaning.
Employment is an uncountable noun which refers in general to the state of having paid work: e.g. *She is looking for employment.|the number of people in employment.*
Profession restricts the meaning to non-manual work, requiring some specialist qualifications, in such areas as medicine, teaching and the law.
A **vocation** is work for which one has a special fitness or ability, and usually one that serves other people or one's religion, such as nursing, teaching or the priesthood.
Someone applies for and is selected for a particular **post** or **position** in an organization, and thus takes up an **appointment**.
The term **job** is the usual informal word for regular paid work: e.g. *I've got a good job*; but can sometimes be derogatory: e.g. *I enjoy my work well enough, but for me it's just a job.* (i.e. I do it

for the money, not out of a sense of vocation.)
△ △ 496–7

C The word is **free**.
Free speech is the right to express your personal opinions, particularly your political views, in public.
If you give someone a **free hand**, you give them freedom of action and let them take the decisions.
Free-range chickens are chickens kept under natural conditions, for example in a farmyard, rather than in small boxes or batteries.
Free will is the power to decide freely what one will and will not do, including the freedom to make mistakes.
A **free-for-all** is an argument or fight in which everybody joins in.
** 411–2

D Since the first milestone is one mile away from the start of the road, Sue won because she only had to walk five miles.

E One's breath **comes in short pants**, that is, in short, quick breaths, after strenuous exercise.

F It was late when their parents got back and the children were already **fast** asleep (in a deep sleep).

G Depending on how good your mechanic is, it might **cough, splutter, roar, purr, tick over**, or even – if you are unlucky – **pink**.

Counter- generally indicates opposing or opposite in direction, but can also mean matching.

Of the words given, the following may take the prefix counter-: counterpoint is the combination of two or more tunes so that they can be played together as a single whole; a counterfoil is the part of a cheque or money order kept by the sender as a record; a counterclaim is usually a legal term for an opposing claim; a countermeasure is an action taken to oppose another action or situation: e.g. *the Government's countermeasures against terrorism*; a counterblast is a violent or angry reply: e.g. *Her article provoked a quick counterblast from other newspapers*; to countersign is to sign a paper already signed by someone else; and a countertenor is a male singer with a high voice or the voice itself.
** B7

3 The missing word is inch.
Not budge an inch means not to change one's mind, however much people try to persuade you.
Give someone an inch and they'll take a mile means that if you allow someone a little freedom or power, they'll try to take a lot more.

C A black hole is an astronomical term for an area in outer space which pulls into itself everything around it, including light.
Black magic is magic used for evil purposes with the help of evil spirits.
Blackmail is the act of obtaining money by threatening to make known unpleasant facts about someone.
The black market (which thrives on black money) is illegal trading involving the avoidance of taxes or state controls.
The black sheep of the family is the member (many families have one) who is considered by the others to be a failure or to have brought shame on the family.
A black spot on the roads is one at which there is a high risk of accident.
And there are many others: a black mark for you if you can't find any!
** 94–5

D One connection could be drop: raindrop and dropout.

E The word is blow.

F I've been working since five o'clock this morning and I'm tired out.
Tired is followed by out to mean extremely tired.

G The full list is: New Year's Day; Good Friday; Easter Monday; Early May Bank Holiday; Spring Bank Holiday; Summer Bank Holiday; Christmas Day; Boxing Day. A busman's holiday is one spent doing one's usual work.

A Here are some possibilities; a **dead end** is the end of a road with no way out; a **dead-end** job is one that leads nowhere; in a **dead heat**, two competitors in a race finish at exactly the same time. A **deadline** in a schedule is a date by which something has to be done – most of us miss our deadlines but they are a wonderful discipline anyway. If you have (or wear) a **deadpan** expression, your face shows no emotion, especially when you are telling jokes (compare a **poker face** – ** 795). **Dead wood**, apart from the obvious, refers to useless people or things: a new manager of an organization often starts by *cutting out the dead wood*. And you can be **dead** certain, **dead** pleased or **dead** miserable – where **dead** means 'completely'. ** 262

B Some possibilities are: **Great! Wonderful! Fantastic! Splendid! Superb! Tremendous! Enchanting! Out of this world!** – and there are many more.
△ △ 247–8

C The word is **head**.
A dreamer, an impractical person, has his or her **head in the clouds**. You do well to **keep your head**, that is, to keep calm, in **a crisis**. Problems sometimes **come to a head**, that is, they reach the point where a decision must be made. You shouldn't let success (if you've got all these right) make you proud and conceited – or **go to your head**!

D To be quite certain, she had to take seven.

E You can **let yourself go** in two very different senses. You may let yourself relax and enjoy things, a a party, for example, or you may fail to look after your health, you figure, your clothes, etc. Clearly, an invitation to **let yourself go** is meant in the first sense.
** 600

F The expression is **soaked to the skin**, so:

The rainstorm caught us unawares and we were soaked to the skin.

G A **delegate** is someone who has been appointed to speak, vote or take decisions for a group, at a meeting, seminar or conference, for example, and a **delegation** is a group of such delegates.
A **congregation** is a group of people gathered together for religious worship, especially in a church.
A **jury** is a group of twelve people chosen to hear all the details of a case in a court of law and give their decision on whether someone is innocent or guilty.
Supporters form a group of people who attend football matches, political meetings, etc., in order to give vocal encouragement to a particular team or group.
An **audience** is a group of people listening to or watching a performance of some kind.

They are all part of the language of legal documents. **Hereafter** means after this time; **hereby** means by means of this statement, law, etc.; **herein** means in this piece of writing; **heretofore** means until now, before this time; **hereupon** means at or after this point in time; and **herewith** means with this letter or written material.

Addition means the act of adding, or something added: e.g. *With the addition of another room, the house is now quite large.*

Adjacent means very close, touching or almost touching: e.g. *The new offices are adjacent to the public library.*

Adverse means unfavourable, going against: e.g. *The architect's plans for the square have provoked a great deal of adverse comment.*

The noun **address**, apart from referring to the number of one's house and the name of one's street and town, also means a formal speech made to a group of people: e.g. *The president's address was not particularly well received.*

The noun **advocate** refers to a person, especially a lawyer, who speaks in defence of, or in favour of, another person, or anyone who speaks in favour of an idea or cause: e.g. *She has, throughout her life, been a strong advocate of religious toleration.*

To **adhere** to means to stick something firmly, with glue for example, or to continue to follow or remain loyal to an idea, belief or plan: e.g. *She continued to adhere to her principles despite*

enormous pressure to conform. There are many other words beginning with **ad-**, such as **adduce, admit, adapt**, and so on.
** 10–15

C Someone who **carries the can** is the one who takes the blame when something goes wrong: e.g. *All right, I'll go along with the plan, but who carries the can if it doesn't work?*
Someone who **carries weight** has influence: e.g. *Her arguments carry a lot of weight with the voters.*
Someone who **carries things too far** does something for too long or to too great a degree: e.g. *He sometimes carries practical jokes too far and someone gets hurt.*

D One possibility is **pass**, to make **underpass**, which is a road built under another road or a railway line, and **passport**.

E You can't make it **drink**, according to the proverb which claims that the most one can do is to provide opportunities for people; whether they take advantage of them or not is their own decision.

F We've done everything we can. Now all we can do is hope for the best and keep our **fingers** crossed.
To **keep one's fingers crossed** means to hope.

G When we talk about temperature **C** refers to **Celsius** or **Centigrade**, a scale on which water boils at 100 degrees and freezes at 0 degrees. **F** refers to the **Fahrenheit** scale, on which water boils at 212 degrees and freezes at 32 degrees.

A Obvious examples are
**headmaster, headline, headlight,
headquarters**, and **heading**, where
head- suggests top position or
prominence, or words such as
headphones and **headrest**, where
head- obviously refers to the part
of the body itself.
** 484–5

B The parts are as follows:

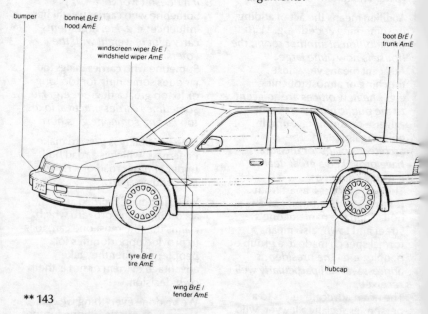

bumper

bonnet *BrE* /
hood *AmE*

windscreen wiper *BrE* /
windshield wiper *AmE*

boot *BrE* /
trunk *AmE*

tyre *BrE* /
tire *AmE*

wing *BrE* /
fender *AmE*

hubcap

** 143

C The missing word is **hair**.
Your **hair** is said to **stand on end**
when you are frightened.
You **let your hair down** when you
lose your inhibitions and relax (at
a party, for example).
To **not turn a hair** is to show no
fear, surprise or nervousness.
To **split hairs** is to introduce
unimportant differences into
arguments.

D One possibility is **some**, to make
wholesome and **something**.

E The word is **sentence**, which is
both a group of words, and also
the punishment handed out by a
judge.

F Grace appreciates most kinds of
music, but jazz isn't really her **cup
of tea**.
One's cup of tea is the sort of
thing one likes.

G **Oxbridge** is used to mean of or
from the universities of Oxford
and/or Cambridge. **Oxon** means
of Oxford University and is used
after the title of a degree: e.g.
Mary Smith, MA Oxon. **Cantab** is
used in the same way after a
Cambridge degree.

A As well as the more obvious combinations, such as **hard-boiled** (which we met in Unit 3), **hard-hearted** and **hard luck**, note the following expressions: a **hard-bitten** person has been made firm and strong by long and hard experience, as in *a hard-bitten old soldier*; a **hard-nosed** person is extremely determined, firm and practical in behaviour: *a hard-nosed businessman*; a **hard nut** (to crack) is a difficult person or thing to deal with; and if you are **hard up** you haven't enough money.

B It's difficult to make noises on paper! The meanings are as follows. A **hiccup** is a sudden sharp sound caused by a movement in the chest which stops the breath. To **sniffle** is to sniff repeatedly to prevent fluid from coming down the nose, especially when one is crying or suffering from a cold. A **sneeze** is a sudden uncontrolled burst of air out of the nose. To **cough** is to push air out from the throat suddenly with a short rough sound, especially because of discomfort in the throat during a cold or other infection. **Hiccups**, **sniffles**, **sneezes** and **coughs** are all to some extent involuntary noises, **hm** and **tut tut** are not. **Hm** is a short humming sound made with closed lips. In English it signals that the person who makes it has doubts about or disagrees with what has just been said, or needs time to think about it. **Tut tut** is a sound like a /t/ made by sucking in rather than forcing air out, to produce a clicking sound. In English it tends to signal slight annoyance or disapproval.
△△ B117

C To **fall foul of** someone is to quarrel, fight or get into trouble with them.
If an idea **falls flat** it fails. If a joke **falls flat** nobody is amused by it. If you would **fall over backwards** to be able to do something you would be tremendously eager, and try everything you possibly could to achieve your wish.

D One possibility is **over**, which would make **Passover**, the Jewish holiday in memory of the escape of the Jews from Egypt, and to **overplay**, to make something appear more important than it is.

E In the well-worn idiom, from the sky: **It's raining cats and dogs**.
** 857

F **Sweet** contrasts with **sour** in Chinese food, such as sweet and sour fish. **Sweet** contrasts with **savoury** to describe the two main types of dish: dishes made with salt, cheese, meat or vegetables, without sugar, are **savoury**, while dishes made with sugar such as cakes, pies and puddings are **sweet**. **Sweet** contrasts with **bitter** to describe certain drinks, especially medicine. **Sweet** contrasts with **dry** when referring to wines.

G **Pickled peppers**, according to a well-known tongue twister (a word or phrase that is difficult to speak quickly or correctly). Here are two more examples of tongue twisters. See how quickly and correctly you can say them:
Red leather, yellow leather, red leather, yellow leather (repeat three times).
She sells sea shells on the sea shore (repeat three times).

A Here are the correct words:
officialdom is an often derogatory reference to officials as a group; a **likeness** is a resemblance: e.g. *Can you see the likeness between her and her father?*; **likelihood** means probability: *There's little likelihood of rain today*; **childhood** is the state or time of being a child; **martyrdom** is the death or suffering of a martyr; and **meanness** is the state, act or habit of being unwilling to give or share what one has.

B If you had plenty of time, you could **amble, saunter**, or **stroll**. If you were in a hurry you could **march, pace** or **stride**. If you didn't want to be noticed you might **creep, sneak** or even **tiptoe**. And if you were injured or handicapped in some way you might **hobble** or **limp**.

C In addition to the straightforward ones such as **blood count, blood group, blood heat** and so on, note the following more unusual combinations: a **blood-and-thunder** film or story is one which is full of exciting action and meaningless violence; a **blood relation** is a person related by birth rather than by marriage; and **bloodstock** describes horses that have been bred for racing.
** 99–100

D One possibility is **age**, to make **manage** and **ageless**.

E Figuratively speaking, when we **take something with a pinch of salt** we remain doubtful about it and don't completely believe it: e.g. *You've got to take what Geoffrey says with a pinch of salt. He's not a liar but he loves to tell a good story.*

F **Strong** is a general word which may be applied to most things. **Mighty** is a more literary word which means great in power, size or strength, and can be used particularly of people, nations and natural phenomena. **Powerful** means able to produce great physical force, great in effect, or having much control and influence. **Brawny** has the narrowest meaning, perhaps, as muscular and is usually only used of people's physical appearance. So the appropriate combinations are:

strong – tea, ruler, wrestler (and to a lesser extent torch)
mighty – ruler, wrestler
powerful – ruler, torch, wrestler
brawny – wrestler (and possibly ruler)

G A large tent; a ring; a variety of animals performing tricks; clowns; jugglers; acrobats; high-wire artists; trapeze artists; and a ring-master.
** 174

Downstream means moving with the current of a river or stream; **downcast** means sad and dejected; **downwind** means in the direction that the wind is moving; someone **down-at-heel** is dressed in old worn-out clothes whose condition suggests lack of money; and a person's or group's **downfall** is the thing that causes their ruin or fall from a high position. Other possibilities are: **down-and-out, downbeat, downplay, downpour, downstairs** and **down-to-earth**.
** 307–8

B If it was a good one it might include: **frying** (cooking in hot fat or oil); **boiling** (cooking in water at 100°C [see Unit 21 G]); **stewing** (cooking in liquid in a covered container over a long period); **braising** (cooking slowly in fat and a little liquid in a closed container); **simmering** (cooking in water which is at or just below boiling heat); **poaching** (cooking eggs or fish by simmering); **scrambling** (cooking eggs by beating then heating them in a saucepan with butter and milk); **currying** (stewing with hot spices); **baking** (cooking by using direct heat in an oven); **roasting** (cooking by using heat in or from a fire, or by baking uncovered in an oven); **grilling** (cooking under or over direct heat); **basting** (cooking by adding fat or oil while roasting or grilling); and **barbecuing** (roasting or grilling on a framework over an open fire).
** 226, △△ 228–9

C Here are some possibilities.
A **first night** is the evening on which the first public performance of a play or show is given.
Something **first-class** is of the highest or best quality.
To hear something **first-hand** is to hear it from the person most closely connected with it.
A **first refusal** is the right to decide whether to buy something before it is offered to other people.
First past the post is a system of voting in elections by which the person who gets the most votes in each constituency is elected to parliament.
** 384–5

D

B	A	R
I	C	E
B	E	D

E You wouldn't **trust** them: e.g. *Margaret is very plausible, but personally I wouldn't trust her as far as I could throw her.*

F The sight was so astonishing that people came from the **four** corners of the earth to see it (from everywhere).

G You might ride on big machines such as roundabouts, dodgem cars and the big wheel. You might play games of skill or chance such as the coconut shy, hoop-la or Bingo. You might even have your fortune told by a 'gipsy' and eat a variety of fast foods.
** 422

A A **grandfather clock** is a tall clock which stands on the floor, with a long wooden outer case and the face at the top.

If you have a **grand slam**, you win either all of a set of important sports competitions, or all the card tricks possible at one time, especially in the game of bridge.

A **grand prix** is any of a set of important car races held under international rules.

A **grand master** is a chess player of a very high level of skill.

A **grandstand** is a set of seats, arranged in rising rows and sometimes covered by a roof, from which people watch sports matches or races for example.

A **grand piano** is a large piano with strings set horizontally.

B They all represent the sound of blows, especially in comics.

C **Civil** has the meaning of belonging to or consisting of the ordinary population of citizens and can be joined to many other words to form combinations such as **civil law, civil liberty, civil rights, civil servant** and **civil war**. Note also **civil list**, the sum of money voted yearly by Parliament to the King or Queen as head of state, and to certain other related people.
** 175–6

D

S	O	B
I	R	E
T	E	N

Ire is a literary word meaning 'anger'.
Ore is a rock from which metal can be obtained.

E You might just **miss**, that is, avoid or escape from, something unpleasant, such as being hit or hurt by something, by good fortune: *The lorry driver just missed being killed when his brakes failed. Fortunately there was no other traffic about and he was able to bring the lorry under control.*

You might just **miss the boat/the bus**, that is, lose a good opportunity for a job or business deal, for example, by being too slow: *Helen might have got the Washington job but she spent too long thinking about it. By the time she'd made up her mind to apply they'd given it to Jane so poor old Helen missed the boat/ bus again.*

Or of course you might simply just **miss** a bus, a train or a plane by arriving at the departure point too late.

F What was the **price** of that beautiful watch we saw in the jeweller's shop window? When we talk about the money needed to buy an object the usual word is **price**. **Cost** has a similar meaning but is used more for services or for general things: e.g. *the cost of living*. **Charge** means the sum of money demanded, usually for allowing someone to do something: e.g. *How much do you charge for use of the car park?*

G Dogs, cats, parrots, budgerigars, rabbits, mice and hamsters, among others.
** 768

By the way (** 1191) is an expression used to introduce a new subject in conversation: e.g. *Yes, I agree entirely . . . By the way, are you and Ann joining us this evening?*
A **by-product** is something additional that is formed in the making of something else: e.g. *Silver is often a by-product of the separation of lead from rock.*
By accident means not deliberately, by chance: e.g. *I didn't plan to see Marjorie this afternoon. We met purely by accident.*
By and by (now rather dated) means soon, before long: e.g. *I know it's very painful just now, but by and by you'll forget him.*

B Some possibilities are:

owl	dog	cat
blackbird	fox	lion
thrush	wolf	tiger
cuckoo	dingo	leopard
sparrow	jackal	panther
starling		cheetah

horse	cow	snake
donkey	ox	lizard
ass	bullock	crocodile
mule	buffalo	alligator
	steer	chameleon
	bull	

C Class may mean a social group whose members have the same social, political and economic position and rank: e.g. *the upper classes/the working class.* It may refer to categories of living things, such as animals, fish or reptiles: e.g. *The crocodile is the largest example of the reptile class.* It can be used to describe a group of pupils or students who are taught together: e.g. *Maria and John are both in my class this year.* Or it can refer to the subject pupils are being taught: e.g. *I've got an English class at two o'clock.* **Class** is also used to describe a stylish quality, in clothes or social behaviour, that attracts admiration: e.g. *Giovanna has really got class.*

D

L	A	P
O	D	E
T	O	N

Ado means delay: *Without more ado, I'll introduce our main speaker for this evening.*
When you are sitting your **lap** is the front part of your body between your waist and your knees; **to lap** means to drink by quick movements of the tongue: e.g. *The cat began to lap the warm milk.*
An **ode** is a long poem addressed to a person or thing. A **ton** is a measure of weight.

E **Procrastination** is the thief of time (according to Edward Young [1683–1765] in his 'Night Thoughts').

F The expression is **at a guess**, so: I'm not sure of his age but, **at a guess**, I'd say he was about thirty.

G **Conkers** is a traditional British game, played in pairs, in which one child tries to defeat the other by breaking his or her **conker** (a horse chestnut tied to a string) with his or her own conker.

A A **crossbar** is a bar joining two upright posts, especially two goalposts.

Cross-country means across the fields or open country.

To **cross-examine** is to question someone, for example, a witness, very closely, usually in order to compare the answers with other answers given before.

Cross-legged means having the knees wide apart and the ankles crossed.

If two people are **at cross-purposes** they misunderstand each other; i.e. they are actually talking about different things but believing that they are talking about the same thing.

A **crossroads** is a place where two or more roads cross.

A **cross-section** is a surface made by cutting across something, especially at right angles to its length.

A **crossword**, or crossword puzzle, is a printed game in which words are fitted into a pattern of numbered squares in answer to numbered clues, in such a way that words can be read across as well as down when the pattern is completed.

B You **knit**, that is, you make things to wear such as sweaters, scarves and gloves, by joining woollen threads into a fabric with long **knitting needles**.

To **sew** is to join or fasten pieces of cloth by stitches made with a sewing **needle** and **thread**.

To **embroider** is to make a decorative needlework picture or pattern on a piece of cloth with a needle and a thread.
△△ 443

C A **common** is a piece of grassland with no fences where people are free to roam: e.g. *We often used to walk together across the common.*

To be **common (to)** means to be shared by more than one person: e.g. *The village well is common to all the villagers.*

Something **common** is found or happens often in many places: e.g. *It's quite common these days for young people to be unemployed.*

Common also means 'ordinary': *common salt*; and 'vulgar': *a common-looking person*.

As a technical term **common** means 'having the same relationship to two or more quantities': e.g. *5 is a common factor of 10 and 20.*

D There are three, six, and nine zeros respectively.

E The missing words are **a crowd**. This expression is used when a third person is not wanted by two people who are happy together.
** 1145

F The correct expression is **on leave** (on holiday).

Our eldest son is in the navy, but at present he's at home **on** leave.

G The sentence usually continues **there was** . . . or **there were** . . . This is a standard introduction to children's stories, which signals to the listeners that they are entering the world of make-believe: *Once upon a time there was a little girl no bigger than your thumb . . .*

The word is **full**.
If you ask for **full board** in a hotel, you are given all your meals.
Something or someone who comes **full circle** goes through several changes or developments and ends up back at the starting point.
A **full face** photograph or painting shows a front view of someone's face.
A **full-grown** animal or plant is completely developed.
A full theatre or cinema is called a **full house**.
A **full-length** photograph or painting shows all of a person, from head to foot; a **full-length** garment reaches the ground.
A **full moon** is completely round.
A **full-scale** model or drawing is the same size as the object it represents.
A **full stop** is the point which marks the end of a sentence.
To work **full-time** is to work the complete number of hours of the usual working period.

B It all depends on whom we are describing and how polite we want to be. (Rather) **overweight** is more polite than **fat**. **Plump** is more often used of women and children and means slightly (and pleasantly) fat. **Stout** means rather fat and heavy and **tubby** means short and rather fat, especially in the stomach. If someone is extremely fat and unhealthy they are said to be **obese**.

C Apart from the most common senses of smooth, level, not thick or high, **flat** also has the following meanings.
A **flat** is a set of rooms in a building, especially on one floor,

including kitchen and bathroom.
A **flat** sound in music is lower than the stated note by a semitone.
Flat beer or other gassy drinks are no longer fresh because the gas has been lost.
Flats are a low level plain, usually near water.
There are several other senses which you can find on ** 389.

D ... call **on Don**ald ... tri**p a ris**ky ... climb **on,** naturally ... a **mad** ri**de** ... **at hens** ... 'Go slow!' ... A he**ro? Me?** ...

E According to the proverb, **Time and tide wait for no man**.

F To **refuse** and to **decline** both mean that you do not do something that you are asked to do. **Decline** is rather more polite than **refuse**, and is used of an offer or request. To **reject** means to refuse to accept, consider, or use. So the possibilities are:

I regret that I must **decline** your invitation.
The horse **refused/rejected** the apple that Pat had brought for her.
Despite our protests, we were **refused** permission to film the event.
The proposals were **rejected** without further discussion.
Do you intend to **decline/reject** their offer then?

G The number 999 in Britain is an emergency telephone number which may be dialled free of charge by anyone requiring the police, fire brigade or ambulance service. The operator asks which service is required, and then connects the caller.

A A **French bean** is a long thin green bean.
French mustard is a hot yellow condiment used to add taste to meat (rather milder than the fierce English version).
French dressing is a liquid made of oil and vinegar, used on salads.
French polish is a liquid rubbed on wooden furniture to give a hard and lasting shine.
French windows are a pair of light outer doors made of glass in a frame, usually opening onto the garden of a house.

B A **grocer** sells dry and preserved foods, sugar, flour, tea, matches and other household requirements such as toiletries. A **greengrocer** sells fruit and vegetables. A **butcher** sells meat. A **baker** sells bread and pastries. An **ironmonger** sells hardware, especially metal goods such as pans and tools. A **department store** sells almost everything.

C The missing word is **heart**.
'They **didn't have the heart to** leave him behind' means they didn't have the courage, firmness or hardness of heart to leave him.
'She had **set her heart on** a new bicycle' means she wanted a new bicycle very badly and was expecting to get one.
'His **heart is in the right place**' means he is a kind person and his intentions are good, although he may seem rough or rude on the outside.

D The word is **season**, which means both to give special taste to a food by adding salt, pepper or spices and also spring, summer, autumn and winter.

E To **turn a blind eye** to something is to pretend not to notice it even though it may be illegal or socially unacceptable: e.g. *The management tends to turn a blind eye to petty pilfering but will not tolerate stealing.*

F **Reach, arrive** and **get** are perhaps best distinguished by the preposition, or absence of it, before a noun. **Reach** requires no preposition, **arrive** takes **at/in** and **get** takes **to**. Thus:

When they **got to** the airport the plane had already left.
By the time I **reached** the front of the queue they had almost sold out.
We're not going to **get** (or possibly **arrive**) back home until morning at this rate.
You're due to **arrive** in New York at about eight.
She **reached** the conclusion that he didn't know what he was talking about.

Note, however, before **there**, all three are possible:
When they **arrived/reached/got** there they were exhausted.

G You would probably say **sh** or **SSH**!
** 959

The suffix **-proof** in adjectives means treated or made so as not to be harmed by something. In verbs it means to treat or make in this way. You may think of **waterproof, shockproof, bulletproof** and **burglarproof** as well as **childproof** (for medicines and locks on rear doors of cars). ** B14

To a British person the **Continent** normally means the rest of Europe.
The **Middle East** refers to the countries in Asia west of India, such as Iran, Iraq and Syria.
The **Far East** refers to the countries in Asia east of India, such as China and Japan.
The **New World** refers to the Americas.
The **Third World** refers to the industrially less developed countries of the world.
The **Commonwealth** is an organization of independent states which were formerly parts of the British Empire, established to encourage trade and friendly relations among its members.

C At **crack of dawn** means very early in the morning.
The **crack of doom** means the end of the world.
A **fair crack of the whip** is a fair chance of doing something.

D The word is **corn**, which is both a type of grain plant and a painful area of thick hard skin on the foot, usually on or near a toe.

E Someone who hasn't got **two pennies to rub together**, or is **broke**, has no money.

F Let us raise our glasses and drink **to** Gillian and Robert.
The young woman drank **in** the professor's words eagerly.
Come on everybody, drink **up**. It's time to go.

We **drink to** a person whom we honour or wish good luck to.
We **drink in** the words of someone we admire.
To finish one's drink is to **drink up**.

G All these expressions are connected with banking.
A **current account** is a bank account which does not usually earn a high rate of interest and from which money can be taken out at any time.
A **deposit account** is a bank account intended for saving money which earns interest, and from which money can often only be taken out if advance notice is given.
A **crossed cheque** is a cheque with two lines drawn across it which may only be paid into the account of the person whose name is written on the top line after the word 'Pay'.
A **cheque card** in Britain is a small plastic card given by a bank to those who have an account with it, which promises that the bank will pay the amount written on their cheques, up to a certain limit.
A **cash card** is another plastic card which enables the holder to obtain money from a cash dispensing machine outside the bank.
A **Eurocheque card** works like a normal British cheque card but may also be used in several countries in Europe.

A Apart from common ones such as **Red Cross, Red Crescent** and **red-hot** (of metal), note the following. To be caught **red-handed** is to be caught in the act of doing something wrong; a **red herring** is a fact or subject which is introduced to draw people's attention away from the main point; and the expression **red tape** refers to silly detailed unnecessary official rules that delay action.
** 870–71

B An owl **hoots**; a dog **barks**; a cat **mews** or **miaows**; a horse **neighs** or **whinnies**; a cow **moos**; and a snake **hisses**.
△△ 10

C You might consider **boarding school** (a school at which pupils live); **boardinghouse** (a private lodging house, not a hotel, that supplies meals); and **boarding card** (an official card to be given up when one enters an aircraft).

D The words are **knead** (to press dough repeatedly in the making of bread), and **need**.

E You would do this when you were exactly right in words or action: e.g. *You've hit the nail on the head. That's exactly what we ought to do.*

F **Great, large, big** and **huge** all mean of more than average size.
Large is slightly more formal than **big**.
Great means famous or important when we are talking about people and very large and impressive when we are talking about things.
Huge means extremely large. So I'm afraid I shall have to take this skirt back to the shop. It's a bit too **big** for me.

G A great deal depends on the age of the speaker, as well as the circumstances, but here is a rough guide:
A **baby** is a very young child, especially one who has not yet learnt to walk or speak.
A **boy** is a young male person.
A **girl** is a young female person. [Note: Many people feel that it is offensive to call a woman a girl after she has become an adult.]
A **youth** is a young person, especially a male teenager; the word is often used in the press to refer to young people who have been involved in some kind of trouble making or criminal activity.
A **young man** or **woman** is a person from the age of 16–18 until approximately 40.
Middle-aged describes the period between youth and old age, roughly from 40 to 60, but this period is very flexible and one's behaviour is often the deciding factor.
The same is often true of **old man** and **old woman**, but **OAP (old age pensioner)** in Britain refers to men over 65 and women over 60 who are entitled to be paid a pension by the state, having reached the required age to stop working.

You might be 100 metres above **sea level** (the average height of the sea).

You would eat **seafood** (fish and fish-like animals) out of shells.

You might like to be beside the **seaside** (in the words of an old song).

You might look for flotsam and jetsam (broken unwanted things washed up by the sea) on the **seashore**.

There are plenty of expressions to choose from here: **terrible, atrocious, revolting, awful, appalling, horrible, unbelievably bad**, and so on.
△ △ 249–50

C You might think of the following: **from the cradle to the grave** means from birth till death; to **dig one's own grave** is to cause one's own ruin, failure or death; to **have one foot in the grave** is to be very old and near death; **as silent as the grave** means completely silent; if someone who is dead is said to **turn in** his or her **grave** it means that they would be very annoyed or worried if they were still alive: e.g. *If old George knew what the new owners had done to his house he'd turn in his grave.*

D The words are **Greece** (the

country) and **grease** (an oily substance).

E Here are a few examples: to **not take one's eyes off** something means never to stop watching it; to **keep one's eyes open** or **peeled** means to watch carefully; to **have eyes in the back of one's head** means to be able to see or notice everything; to **keep an eye on** is to watch carefully; **one in the eye for** someone is a disappointment or defeat for someone; **with half an eye** means without looking or inquiring closely; and to do something **with one's eyes open** means to do it knowing fully what the problems, difficulties or results might be.
** 359

F Doctors are now firmly convinced that cigarettes are bad **for** your health.

The expression is **bad for** or **good for**. Note also the Australian phrase **good on you**, expressing approval of someone.

G You would address the audience in a formal speech as **ladies and gentlemen**. An ambassador is addressed as **Your Excellency**; a prince or princess as **Your Highness**; a president as **Mr/ Madam President**; and a prime minister as **Prime Minister**.
** 11

A The suffix **-ish** has four meanings. In nouns and adjectives it may mean the people or language belonging to a stated country or place: *British/Spanish*. It may also be used derogatively to mean 'like a —' in such expressions as: '*Don't be foolish/childish*'. It may also have the meaning of 'to some degree, rather, quite', as in: *She's tallish, with reddish hair*. And another meaning is 'approximately', as in: *Come at eightish* (at about eight o'clock). So it is really a most versatile suffix and many words are possible.
** B12

B All these words share the sense of 'to have an unpleasant disagreement in which people feel angry.'
To **argue** can also mean to have a discussion in which there are differences of opinion.
To **quarrel** is to argue angrily, often about something not very important.
To **squabble** and to **bicker** both mean to quarrel, especially about unimportant matters.
To **fall out** has the same meaning, informally, as **quarrel**, with the implication sometimes of semipermanence.
To **disagree** is to have different opinions, to quarrel slightly.
△△ 259

C The missing word is **way**. 'He **has a way with** children' means he has an attractive quality which persuades or pleases them. 'She always **gets** her **own way**' means she always persuades people to do or to let her do as she wishes. 'I want to **pay my way**' means I want to pay for things as I buy them and not get into debt. 'You'd better **mend your ways**' means you'd better improve your behaviour or work. 'He's very **set in his ways**' means he has very fixed habits.

D The two words are **bough** (branch of a tree) and **bow** (to incline the head and/or the upper body).

E You may **break the ice** in many ways – with music, dancing, drinks, games, conversation, and so on. The expression means to remove feelings of awkwardness or nervousness, especially between people who do not know each other.

F Mrs Evans is **on** the phone at the moment.
To **be on the phone** can mean either to have a telephone in one's home or to be speaking to someone by telephone.
At the phone might be a possibility here if the phone in question was a public one outside the building where the remark was made.

G

C	L	E
Cambridge	Leeds	Exeter
Coventry	Leicester	Ely
Canterbury	Lancaster	East
Chesterfield	Liverpool	Kilbride
Colchester	Luton	Eastleigh

Although 'second-foot shoes' is an unacceptable coinage, it is nevertheless possible to combine **second** with a number of other words. You may think of: **second best** (not as good as the best); **second-hand** (not new); **second-rate** (of low quality); **second sight** (the ability to see or know about future or far-away things); **second thought** (a thought that a past decision or opinion may not be right); and **second nature** (a very firmly fixed habit).
** 943

The odd ones out (the one different from the rest of each group) are:

Exeter – the others are all ports
carbon – the others are all metals
yew – the others are all deciduous trees (their leaves fall off in autumn)
trout – the others are all salt-water fish
liver – the others are all names for the meat of specific animals

C The missing word is **right**.
He isn't **right in the head** means he's mad.
She's **right as rain** means she's perfectly healthy.
Right enough means of an acceptable standard.
Right you are and **Right oh**! are both colloquial ways of agreeing to do as someone suggests.

Quite right! expresses emphatic agreement.

D The two words are **right** and **write**.

E Not really. The proverb suggests that '**a stitch in time saves nine**,' not three. It means it is better to sort out problems quickly, when it is still easy to do so, otherwise they will get worse and be much harder to deal with.

F **Reason, pretext** and **excuse** cover the same general area, but they have slight differences in meaning.
A **reason** is a fact, event, or statement that provides an explanation or excuse for something.
An **excuse** is a reason, which may be true or untrue, given to ask forgiveness for something.
A **pretext** is a false excuse.

George just couldn't stand the office any more so he left early on the **pretext** that his daughter was sick. (She WASN'T sick really.)
She said she was going to take the dog for a walk, but perhaps that was simply her **excuse** to go to the pub. (It may or may not have been the real reason.)
Ann was better qualified than the other candidates and that's the **reason** why she got the job. (A valid reason.)

G Float like a **butterfly**, sting like a **bee**.
Ali's own words to describe his superb boxing skill.

A The prefix **over-** adds the sense of 'too much'.
Thus to **overact** is to act a part in a play in a way that goes beyond what is natural.
Overage means too old for some purpose.
To **overawe** someone is to make them quiet out of respect or fear.
To **overdraw** is to take more money out of one's bank account than it contains.
To **overdress** is to wear clothes which are too formal.
To **overplay** is to make something appear more important than it really is.
** B9 & 733–6

B A **solicitor** is a lawyer who advises customers on matters of law, appears in the lower courts, and prepares written agreements and cases for the higher courts.
A **barrister** is a lawyer who has the right of speaking and arguing in the higher courts of law.
A **juror** is one of twelve people chosen to hear all the details of a case in a court of law and give their decision on it.
A **magistrate** is an official who has the power to judge cases in the lowest courts of law, especially a police court.
A **judge** is a public official who has the power to decide questions brought before a court of law.
△△ 128

C A **match** may be a game or sports event where people compete. It may also refer to a person who is equal to or better than another in strength, ability, etc.: e.g. *He's no match for her at quick decision making.* It is also used for a thing which is like another or is suitable to be put together with another, especially by having a similar colour or pattern: e.g. *The hat and gloves are a perfect match.* In old-fashioned use, it can mean a possible husband or wife: e.g. *My son would be a good match for your daughter.* And, of course, **matches** are the thin sticks used to light fires, cigarettes, etc.

D The two words are **pale** (light-coloured) and **pail** (a bucket).

E **Too many cooks spoil the broth** is a proverb meaning that if too many people are responsible for something it will not be done properly.

F We **bath** to get ourselves clean.
Bathe is another word for swim.
We also use **bathe** meaning to clean something in a medical way and, in more poetic language, to describe the effect of the sun's rays on natural objects. Thus:
Mike and Andi normally take turns to **bath** the baby.
He usually **baths** before he shaves but today was an exception.
That's a nasty cut. You'd better let me **bathe** it with something.
If the sea's still warm enough at four o'clock we'll **bathe** then.
When the sun rises it **bathes** the mountains with gold.

G You might shout '**Hey**' (rather familiar, but perhaps forgivable in the circumstances); or (more appropriately) '**Look out!**' '**Watch out!**'

The prefix **under-** may mean too little, going underneath or less important. Thus an **underestimate** is an estimate which is too small. An **underpass** is a passage, path or road built beneath a road or railway line. To **underrate** is to have too low an opinion of the quality of something. An **underling** is a person of low rank or position in relation to another, and the **undertow** is the current beneath the surface which pulls back towards the sea as a wave breaks on the shore.
** B10 & 1150–52

B This is very much a matter of personal preference of course. You might like **sunny, dry, warm, hot** or even **cold, windy** and **chilly** weather, and perhaps dislike **cloudy, foggy, rainy, wet, humid, damp, foul, freezing** or **stifling** weather.
△△ 556–62

C **Pitch** may refer to a marked out area of ground on which sports such as football are played. When we talk of the **pitch** of a musical note or a human voice, we are referring to its degree of highness or lowness. **Pitch** is also a black substance that is melted into a sticky material for making protective coverings or for filling cracks, especially in a ship, to stop water coming through. A **pitch** can also be a place in a public area, such as a street or market, where someone regularly tries to get money from people who are passing, by

performing or selling things, for example. The same word as a verb also refers to a backward and forward movement of a ship or aircraft: *The small ship pitched violently in the rough sea.*

D The word is **crest** which means both a design on a coat of arms, and the top or highest point of something.

E This expression has nothing to do with either LPs (long-playing records) or the Olympics (where athletic records are set). **Off the record** refers to something said unofficially, which is not to be recorded on tape or in writing, or made public.

F Charlotte takes a delight **in** teasing her little brother. The expression is **to take a delight in** something. The adjective **delighted** can be followed by **by**: e.g. *She was delighted by what she heard*; or by **with**: e.g. *He was delighted with the gift.*

G **Stratford-upon-Avon** is the birthplace of William Shakespeare, and where his plays are regularly performed. **Stonehenge** is a prehistoric monument on Salisbury Plain dating from c. 1500–1400 BC, believed to have religious or astronomical significance. **Wimbledon** is the centre of lawn tennis in Britain. **Hadrian's Wall** is a wall built across the Solway Firth by the Roman Emperor Hadrian (AD 76–138) to keep out warring tribes.

A **Official** refers to a person in a position of power and responsibility; made known publicly.

Officious means too eager to give orders or to offer advice.

Continual means repeated often and over a long period.

Continuous means continuing without interruption, unbroken.

Exceptional means unusual, especially of unusually high quality or ability.

Exceptionable means likely to cause dislike or offence.

Respectful means feeling or showing respect.

Respectable means showing standards of behaviour, appearance and so on which are socially acceptable.

B In addition to **knives, forks** and **spoons** (cutlery), **plates, saucers, cups, mugs**, and **dishes** (crockery), and so on, we might think of **pressure cooker, kettle, dishwasher, scales, can opener, mixer, bread bin, food processor, fish slice, microwave oven**, and many other machines and utensils.
** 577

C You may think of a **power point** (a wall socket for an electric plug); a **point of view** (an opinion); the **points of the compass** (north, south, east and west); a **point of order** (a matter connected with the organization of an official meeting); a **point-to-point** (a horse-race across country from one place to another); **point-blank** (fired from a very close position); or perhaps a **decimal point** in mathematics.
** 793–4

D The word is **chest** (both a large wooden or steel container and the part of the human body containing the heart and lungs).

E You might spend money like **water**.
News might spread like **wildfire**.

F I know there's something strange going on, but I just can't **put my finger on** it at the moment.
The expression is **to put one's finger on** something, which means to find out or show exactly what is happening.

G A **town** is a group of houses, buildings etc. where people live.
A **city** is a very large town with a centre where business goes on and entertainments can be found.
A **village** is a small group of houses.
A **hamlet** is a very small village.
A **district** is a division of a town.
A **ward** is a division of a town for administrative or political purposes: e.g. *The town is divided into four electoral wards for local elections.*
A **suburb** is an outer area of a city where people live and less business is done.
A **quarter** is a part of a city, often typical of certain groups of people: e.g. *the Latin quarter.*
△ △ 100

A The odd man out is **inflammable**, which means 'easy to set on fire'. In all the other words, the prefix **in-** expresses a negative: **not** capable, **not** separable, **not** human.

B You could add: **temple, forehead, eyebrow, eyelashes, nostrils, lips, chin, throat, jaw, cheek.**
** 483

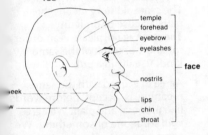

temple
forehead
eyebrow
eyelashes
face
nostrils
cheek
lips
chin
jaw
throat

C The missing word is **well**.
To **do well out of** something is to gain a good profit from it.
To **do well to** do something is to be well-advised to do it.
That **may well be** means that that may be true, but it doesn't alter the situation.
Well and truly means completely.
Oh well is used for showing cheerfulness when something bad has happened.

It's **just as well** (as a reply) means it's fortunate that there's no harm done.
Well! as an exclamation is an expression of surprise.

D The word is **bridge**, which means both a game of cards and a long structure over a road, railway line or river.

E **It**. The expression **it stands to reason** means it (the topic/solution or point made) is clear to all sensible people.

F Mark is a very timid boy. He couldn't say boo to a **goose** (he's very gentle or easily frightened). The expression is **can't/couldn't say boo to a goose**.
** 107

G As well as Hamlet's famous speech 'To be or not to be. That is the question,' this expression may also follow a query in a discussion.

A: *But what about the financial aspects of the merger?*
B: *Yes, that is the question.*
(that's really the biggest problem of all).

A The correct connections are:
unable, impossible, incurious, mistrust, mistake (**intake** is also an English word but without negative meaning), **inevitable, unusual, imperfect**.

B The neutral term is to **preserve**, which means to prepare food for being kept for a long time by some special treatment.
To **smoke** is to dry and preserve meat or fish by hanging them in the rising smoke of wood fires.
To **salt** something is to preserve it by treating it with salt, usually by rubbing it on.
To **cure** meat is to preserve it by smoking, salting or drying it.
To **pickle** food is to preserve it in salt water or vinegar.
And to **freeze** something is, of course, to reduce it to a low or freezing temperature.
△△ 230

C A **racket** may mean a dishonest way of getting money, for example by threatening people or selling them goods which are useless or illegal. It may also mean a loud noise. And it can mean an instrument consisting of a net, usually made of nylon, stretched in a frame with a handle, used for hitting a ball in games such as tennis.

D The word is **bank**, which is both the side of a river or canal and the place where money is kept.

E If two people are **in the same boat** they are both in the same unpleasant situation.
It's not the same without Mabel means that an activity, situation, or even life itself is not as enjoyable as it was with Mabel.
The **same old story** means the usual excuse or difficulty.
The same again, please is an order for another drink of the same kind, usually in a pub.

F **Agree to** is used with the same meaning as 'accept' before words like **proposal** and **plan**. We **agree with** someone or something. We **agree on** a particular point of argument. Thus:
Can I take it that we **agree on** that point at least?
He was reluctant at first but he finally **agreed to** it.
You look wonderful. The Mediterranean obviously **agrees with** you.
Do you all **agree with** what I sugges

G The signs of the zodiac are:
Aquarius, Pisces, Aries, Taurus, Gemini, Cancer, Leo, Virgo, Libra, Scorpio, Sagittarius, Capricorn.
** 1229

A The plurals are: **thieves, sisters-in-law, tomatoes, media** (also **mediums**) and **wolves**.

B To **guffaw**, like to **explode with laughter**, means to laugh loudly.
To **giggle** is to laugh repeatedly in an uncontrolled way (used especially of young girls).
To **titter** is to giggle quietly in a silly or nervous way.
To **chuckle** is to laugh quietly with pleasure or satisfaction.
To **snigger** is to laugh quietly in an unpleasant or rude way.

C If you don't want to be considered old-fashioned you must **move with the times**.
If you are doing all you can to get something done you are **moving Heaven and earth**.
When you've got a new address you have **moved house** (or simply **moved**).

D The word is **host**, which means both a person who receives and entertains guests and a large number.

E No, not necessarily. If a group of people **take turns**, they do something one after the other, instead of all at once.

F **Play** is used with **at** in the fixed expression **What do you think you're playing at?**, used to express annoyance at someone else's behaviour.
To **play with** an idea is to consider it not very seriously.
To **play** something **down** is to make it appear less important than it is.
To **play on** someone's feelings is to try to use them for one's own advantage.
To **play** someone **off** against someone else is to set the two people concerned against each other to one's own advantage.

The appeal **played on** the public's love of animals.
What do you think you're **playing at**? You'll break my machine if you use it like that!
He craftily **played** one friend **off** against the other for his own purposes.
She didn't want to make a fuss, so she **played down** the incident.
Carol is **playing with** the idea of emigrating.

G The **mass media** are newspapers, television and radio.
A **press box** is a space at some outdoor event that is kept for the use of newspaper reporters.
The **gutter press** is a derogatory term for newspapers which tend to be full of deliberately shocking stories about people's personal lives.

KEY 42

A We might consider the following, for example:

A **bookworm** is a person who is very fond, perhaps too fond, of reading and study.

A **bookend** (or more likely a **pair of bookends**) is a support to hold up a row of books.

A **bookmark** is a piece of ribbon, leather or something similar put between the pages of a book to mark a place in it.

Bookbinding is the art of fastening the pages of a book together and enclosing them in covers.

And, finally, **bookish** means fond of books and reading, studious.
** 107

B If left is **port**, then we are talking about a ship or an aircraft. Right is **starboard, fore** is in or towards the front (or **prow**) and **aft** is in or towards the back (or **stern**).
△△ 651

C None of these expressions has necessarily anything to do with a **shop** in the sense of a place where goods are sold.

All over the shop means scattered in disorder, so it could refer to almost anything – books, papers or toys, for example.

To **shut up shop** means to stop doing business, which we might do because it was a public holiday or perhaps simply because we were fed up with doing what we were doing.

It is not usually a good idea to **talk shop**, which means to discuss subjects connected with our work outside business hours. Someone might **shop us**, that is,

inform the police about us, if we had committed a crime.

D The word is **bat**, which means both a winged animal equipped with its own radar system, and any implement with a handle used for striking a ball in, for example, tennis, squash or badminton.

E **Well, I'll be . . .!** is a colloquial expression indicating total surprise. Words to fill the gap may range from the blasphemous or obscene to the relatively mild: *Well, I'll be* **damned/blowed!**

F **High** and **low** are used for measuring things rather than people, especially when we are thinking of distance above the ground. **Tall** is used for people and the opposite is **short**. We can, however, use **tall** for things which are high and narrow: *a* **tall** *building*. **Long** refers to the amount of distance from one end of something to the other, and its opposite is also **short**. For example:

The **low** *range of hills in front of us conceals a much* **higher** *range a few miles beyond it.*
Matthew looks ridiculously **tall** *next to Robin, who's really quite a* **short** *person.*
These trousers are much too **long** *for me. Have you got a* **shorter** *pair?*

G They are all names of independent television networks serving various parts of Britain. **HTV**, for example, stands for **Harlech Television**, representing Wales.

If something can't be done it's **impossible**. If it can't be believed it is **incredible**. Something faultless is **impeccable**. Something which can't be rubbed out is **indelible**. Something which never changes is **immutable**. Someone lacking ability is **incapable**.
You might also think of: **indispensable** (too important or too useful to be without); **indescribable** (impossible to describe); **inevitable** (impossible to avoid); **imperturbable** (remaining calm and steady in spite of difficulties).

B Apart from the words we already met in Unit 31, you might think of the following: A **savings account** is a bank account which earns interest and from which money can usually be taken out only if advance notice is given. A **statement** is a list showing amounts of money paid, received, owing, etc., and their total. To **withdraw** is to take money out of one's bank account. **Credit** is the amount of money in a person's bank account. A **cashier** is a person in charge of money receipts and payments in a bank. To **cash** a cheque or money order means to exchange it for money. And, of course, a **banker** is a person who owns or controls or shares in the control of a bank.
△△ 476–9

C The missing word is **job**.
To **make the best of a bad job** means to do as well as possible in unfavourable conditions.
To **give something up as a bad job** means to decide that something

is impossible and stop trying to do it.
You shouldn't **have much of a job** doing something means it won't be difficult for you.

D The word is **base**, which means both the foundation or bottom part of a building or mountain, for example, and a military installation: *an army base*.

E No. This expression means that someone is not a fool and cannot be tricked: *You can't expect Ms Shoreditch to swallow that excuse. There are no flies on her, you know.*

F The expression is **beast of burden**, which means an animal used for carrying loads. Thus:
The donkey is used in many parts of the world as a beast of **burden**.

G With the exception of **Guy Fawkes' Night** all these days honour saints but are not public holidays in England. **St George's Day** (the patron saint of England) is 23 April. **St Patrick's Day** (patron saint of Ireland) is 17 March. **St Andrew's Day** (patron saint of Scotland) is 30 November. **St Valentine's Day** (in celebration of St Valentine, when people send unsigned cards professing undying love for the recipient) is 14 February. **Guy Fawkes' Night** (named after one of the unsuccessful plotters who intended to blow up the Houses of Parliament in the reign of King James I) is celebrated on 5 November with bonfires and fireworks, and the burning of Guy Fawkes in effigy.

A A **checkup** is a general medical examination, usually taken regularly, to test one's state of health and discover any disease at an early stage.
A **checkout** is a desk in a self-service shop where one pays for goods.
A **checklist** is a complete list, for example of checks to be made or things to be done.
Checkmate in chess is the position of a king at the end of a game when under direct attack, from which escape is impossible.

B You can **gain** something useful or necessary whether or not you deserve it: e.g. *to* **gain** *attention/knowledge/favour*. You can **gain** or **win** something as a result of great effort or ability: e.g. *People disliked him at first, but in the end his willingness to work hard* **gained/won** *their approval*. You can **earn** something which you deserve: e.g. *Take a rest now; you've* **earned** *it*. Or you can earn money for work you do: e.g. *She's* **earning** *£300 a week at present*. To **beat**, especially in sports and games, is to do better than someone else: e.g. *She* **beat** *him at tennis*. To **defeat** has the same meaning as beat, that is, to win a victory over a person or a group: e.g. *Our team* **defeated** *theirs*. The basic pairs are, however:

win – race
defeat – enemies
gain – admission
beat – opponent
earn – reward

C The missing verb is **take in**. 'I just couldn't **take** it all in' means 'I just couldn't fully understand'. 'Could you **take** the dress **in** an inch?' means 'could you make the dress narrower by one inch?' If you **take in** paying guests, you provide lodgings for them. When people are **taken in by** a confidence trickster they are deceived by him or her.

D The word is **race** which means both a running competition, and any of the groups in which people can be categorized according to their physical type.

E No. To **be beside oneself** means to be almost mad or wild with grief or anger.

F There are a number of expressions for the various ways in which letters and parcels may be sent. In Britain we **post** letters; in the USA they are **mailed**. With nouns British usage tends to stick to **post** rather than **mail**: e.g. **parcel post, registered post, postman, post office**, and so on. The main exceptions are **airmail** and **surface mail**. So the sentence should read:

I wanted to be sure the letter arrived in time for Christmas, so I made sure it went **by airmail**.

G This gap may be filled by any number of insulting adjectives, such as the following: silly, stupid, damn, blasted, bloody. Be careful how you use them!

The suffix **-ify** adds the meaning of to make or become, or to fill with. For example, to **clarify** is to make clear, to **falsify** is to make false, to **dignify** is to fill with dignity, to **glorify** is to fill with glory, and to **rectify** is to make correct.

B To **bite** is to cut, crush or seize (something) with the teeth. To **nibble** is to bite gently, with small movements of the mouth. To **chew** is to move and crush something in the mouth with the teeth. To **gnaw** is to bite steadily and continuously on something hard, especially rubbing with the teeth. To **munch** is to chew with strong movements of the mouth, making a noise. To **gobble** is to eat greedily, noisily and quickly. To **tuck in** is to start eating, and to **peck at** is to eat in small amounts, usually without much interest.
△ △ 213–5

C The missing word is **house**. 'The house that Jack built' is part of a children's nursery rhyme. 'The House rose' means that the House of Commons ended its session. 'People who live in glass houses shouldn't throw stones' is a well-known proverb. A **house-trained** dog is one trained to go out of the house to empty its bowels or bladder. To be **house-proud** is to like to have everything in perfect order in the house and to spend a lot of time on keeping it clean and tidy, perhaps too much so.

D The word is **rose**, which is everyone's favourite flower, and is also the past tense of **rise**, to get up.

E You can't take your wealth (it) with you (when you die).

This is usually offered as gratuitous advice to someone who won't spend any money, or as an encouragement to someone who will.

F **Easy** may mean not difficult: e.g. *an easy exam*; comfortable and without worry: e.g. *an easy life*; and pleasant to look at or listen to, in the expression **easy on the eye/ear**. **Simple** may mean, among other senses, plain, not elaborate: e.g. *a simple dress*; easy to understand: e.g. *a simple explanation*; and foolish, easily tricked: e.g. *It may just be a joke to you, but he's simple enough to take it seriously*. Thus:

The home team won an **easy** victory over their opponents.
The **simple** fact is that we can't afford a new car.
Her voice is very **easy** on the ear.
It was just a very **simple** cottage but beautifully furnished.

G All these expressions are connected with the British telephone service.
A **trunk call** is a long-distance call. A **reverse charge** call (**collect call** in the USA) is a call which is paid for by the recipient rather than the caller.
IDD stands for **international direct dialling**. **Directory enquiries** will tell you a person's telephone number if you give his or her name and address (except for **ex-directory** numbers, which are not listed because the people concerned do not want their numbers known to the general public). An **answering machine** records telephone messages automatically when the person called is not present.

A The parts of the body are as follows:

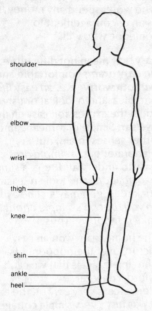

shoulder
elbow
wrist
thigh
knee
shin
ankle
heel

B A **hobby** is an activity which one enjoys doing in one's free time, which could include almost anything. Common hobbies are any kind of sporting activity, or creative activities such as painting, sewing, photography, singing, playing a musical instrument, dancing, amateur dramatics, and collecting various things.
△ △ 507

C We play a musical instrument **by ear** if we don't need to (or cannot) read the music. We learn something, such as a poem, **by heart** if we can recite it from memory. Information is spread **by word of mouth** when it is spread by speaking and not by writing. **By hand** means by a person, not a machine: *written by hand, not typed.*

D The words are **great**, which can sometimes mean large, and **grate**, which can mean to make a sharp unpleasant sound.

E Your boss, because the expression means to work harder with your hands (especially on such tasks as polishing and cleaning).

F All the expressions refer to **measures** of things. The basic pairs are:
a **slice** of **ham** (or bread)
a **puff** of **smoke**
a **drop** of **oil**
a **piece** of **paper**
a **lump** of **sugar**
a **length** of **rope**
a **hunk** of **bread** (or ham)
a **pinch** of **salt** (i.e. an amount that can be picked up between the thumb and finger).
** 776

G **Greenwich Mean Time** is the time at Greenwich, a place in Greater London, which is on an imaginary line dividing east from west. Times in the rest of the world are compared to this and said to be a number of hours earlier or later. **British Summer Time** refers to a period from March to October when clocks in Britain are put forward one hour to save daylight.
Eastern Standard Time is the time on the eastern side of of the USA, five hours later than Greenwich. **European Time** is one hour ahead of Greenwich.
Time zones are the 24 parts into which the earth is divided for the purpose of keeping time.

A The physical parts of a book may include: the **jacket** (a loose paper cover); the **cover** (the hard/soft fixed outer casing); the **spine** (the back part to which the pages are fastened and on which the title is usually printed); and the **pages** themselves. The contents may include the **blurb** (a short description by the publisher of the contents of the book, printed on the cover); the **title**; a **preface** (an introduction to the book); a **foreword** (a kind of preface, especially one in which someone who knows the writer and his work says something about them); the **contents** (a list of what is contained in the printed pages of the book); an **appendix** (a part at the end of the book giving additional information); a **bibliography** (a list of the writings used in the preparation of the book); and an **index** (an alphabetical list of names, subjects, etc. mentioned in the book).
△△ 348

B You may think of **canvassing, election, agent, speaker, leader, prime minister, opposition, platform, heckler, campaign, votes, voters, parties**, and many others.
△△ 109–113

C The missing word is **off**.
You're **off your rocker** means you're mad.
When the waiter in a restaurant tells you a dish (such as steak and kidney pie) is **off**, he means it is not available. Otherwise, when we speak of food being **off**, as in the example: *This fish is going off*, we mean that it is no longer fresh.

To be **off colour** is to be unwell.
And they're off is a set phrase used by a sports commentator to signal that a horse race has begun.
Off you go then is an informal way to tell someone, usually a child or a subordinate, to begin doing what they have been asked to do.

D The words are **seem** which means 'to give the impression of something', and **seam**, a line of stitches joining two pieces of cloth.

E You **work your fingers to the bone** means you work very hard. If you are working hard without a break, you are **keeping your nose to the grindstone**.

F These fixed expressions are as follows:
a **herd** of **cattle**
a **flock** of **sheep**
a **pack** of **wolves**
a **swarm** of **bees**
an **army** of **ants**
a **shoal** of **fish**

G **Hell** (often with a capital letter) is, especially in the Christian and Muslim religions, a place where the souls of bad people are supposed to be punished after death. Otherwise the word has become increasingly common as an expletive and in fixed idioms such as **come hell or high water** (in spite of whatever difficulties might happen); **for the hell of it** (just for fun and no other reason); to **give someone hell** (to treat or speak to someone very angrily); and a few others.
** 489

A The suffix **-ic** in adjectives adds the meaning 'like or connected with'. There are many examples; you might think of **gigantic, horrific, comic, historic, terrific, tragic**, and even **eulogistic**, used of a speech or piece of writing to mean 'full of eulogy or high praise'. In nouns **-ic** means someone on whom the stated thing has an effect, such as an **alcoholic**, and the recent coinage **workaholic**, a person who likes to work too hard or is unable to stop working.
** B12

B Words to fill the bottom slot might include the following: **superb, marvellous, brilliant, wonderful, first class, excellent, out of this world, magnificent** and many others. At the other end of the scale we might find: **awful, terrible, atrocious, appalling, disgusting, disgraceful**, and many more.
△ △ 247–8, 249

C The missing word is **show**.
A **show-off** is a person who behaves so as to try to get attention and admiration for himself or herself or for his or her abilities.
A **show of hands** is a way of voting on an issue by counting the hands raised in favour of an option (or against).
Show business is, of course, the entertainment business, the job of people who work in television, films and the theatre.
Show jumping is a form of horse riding competition judged on ability and often speed in jumping a course of fences.

D The word is **left**, which means both 'remaining': e.g. *There's some cake left* and 'the opposite of right': e.g. *She writes with her left hand.*

E A person, thing or situation that annoys you is **a pain in the neck**.

F Prepositions are not easy to pin down with rules and most uses need to be learnt. **On** is used with the days of the week, **at** with specified times and **in** with the seasons of the year. However, there are special uses such as **at** Oxford, meaning at the University of Oxford, and **in** Oxford, referring to the town itself. Thus:
They'll probably arrive **at** the weekend.
I hope it snows **on** Christmas Day.
The postman normally comes **at** lunchtime.
You can expect reasonably warm weather **in** the spring.
Carol is doing postgraduate research **at** Cambridge now.
We've found a nice little flat **in** Cambridge.

G They are the names of some of the London Underground (Tube) routes. Each route is shown on the map in a different colour.
The **Jubilee** line (silver grey) runs between Stanmore and Charing Cross
The **Bakerloo** line (brown) runs between Harrow & Wealdstone and the Elephant and Castle.
The **Circle** line (yellow) runs in a circle round the central part of the city.
The **Central** line (red) runs between West Ruislip and Ongar.
The **Northern** line (black) runs between High Barnet and Morden.
Why not visit London and try some of these routes?

A **pushcart** is a small cart, pushed by hand, used, for example, by a street tradesman.

A **pushover** is something that is very easy to do or win, or someone who is easy to influence or defeat.

Push-ups (British English **press-ups**) refers to a form of exercise in which someone lies face down on the ground, keeping their back straight, and pushes their body up with their arms.

Push-button describes something operated with a button that one presses with the finger.

A **pushchair** is a small chair on wheels for transporting a small child.

Push off is a rude way of telling someone to go away.

B **Ability** means the power, knowledge or other qualities that are needed to do something.

Skill is a special ability to do something well, especially as gained by learning and practice.

Genius is a very strong word, used only of great and rare powers of thought, skill, or imagination, or of the person who has them.

Talent is less strong, and is used of special natural ability or skill, especially artistic ability.
△ △ 31

C The missing word is **foot**.

To **put one's foot in it** is to say something wrong or unsuitable usually as a result of thoughtlessness, and so cause an awkward situation.

To **put one's best foot forward** is to walk as fast as possible.

To be **footloose and fancy free** is to be free to go wherever one pleases and do what one likes, having no family or business duties to limit one's freedom.

To **foot the bill** is to pay the bill.

D The two letters are **TP (tepee)**.
** 1091

E No. If you **haven't a leg to stand on** you have no support for your position in an argument or discussion.

F **By** is used before people or things that do a job, whereas **with** is used before the things that someone uses to do the job, or the people that accompany them. Thus:

The old man was killed **by** a heavy wooden beam. (An accident resulting from a falling wooden beam.)

The old man was killed **with** a heavy wooden beam. (Someone used a heavy wooden beam as a weapon.)

She was driven to the station **with** her daughter. (Someone drove them both to the station.)

She was driven to the station **by** her daughter. (Her daughter did the driving.)

G St. = Street
Rd. = Road
Ave. = Avenue
Terr. = Terrace
Boul. = Boulevard.
Check the pronunciations in LDOCE.

A The missing prefix is **para-**, which may mean beyond, similar to, or connected with, and helping.
A **paragraph** is a division of a piece of writing which is made up of one or more sentences and begins a new line.
A **parasite** is a plant or animal that lives on or in another and gets food from it.
Paratroops are soldiers trained to drop from an aircraft using a **parachute**.
Paramount means greater than all others in importance or influence.
A **paraphrase** is a restatement in different words of something written or said.
Paraphernalia refers to small articles of various kinds, especially personal belongings or those needed for a particular activity.

B You may wish to include, if you can: **great-grandfather** and **great-grandmother**, your **great-aunt** and **great-uncle**, your **grandmother** and **grandfather**, your **mother**, **father**, **uncle**, **aunt**, **mother-in-law**, **father-in-law**, **husband**, **wife**, **cousins**, **sister-in-law**, **brother-in-law**, **son**, **daughter**, **daughter-in-law**, **son-in-law**, **grandson**, **granddaughter**, **great-grandson**, **great-granddaughter**. If you wish to talk about more distant generations you can simply add **great-** for each: e.g. *my great-great-great-grandmother.*
** 367

C The missing word is **penny**.
'**A penny for your thoughts**' is usually said to someone who has been silent for a while or appears deep in thought. It means: 'Tell me what you're thinking about'.
'To **keep turning up like a bad penny**' is to keep appearing at the most inopportune times.
'It cost me a **pretty penny**' means it was very expensive.
Pennies from Heaven refers to unexpected bonuses or gifts.

D The word is **last**, which is both a piece of wood or metal shaped like a human foot used by shoemakers to repair or make shoes and, of course, the opposite of **first**.

E 57 − 34 = 23 Fifty-seven minus thirty-four equals/is/ makes twenty-three.
10 × 10 = 100 Ten times ten is/equals/makes a hundred.
60 ÷ 6 = 10 Sixty divided by six equals/is/makes ten.
7,435 + 7 = 7,442 Seven thousand, four hundred and thirty-five plus seven is/equals/makes seven thousand, four hundred and forty-two.
** B1

F The offspring of the animals in question are as follows:

dog – puppy   cat – kitten
elephant – calf   sheep – lamb
goat – kid   lion – cub
frog – tadpole   deer – fawn
horse – foal

G **MP** – Member of Parliament
PM – Prime Minister
mpg – miles per gallon
pm – post meridiem (in the afternoon)
PMG – Post Master General (a person who is in charge of a national postal system)
mph – miles per hour